S E R I E S

A life-changing encounter
with God's Word from the book of

EXODUS

NAVPRESS

A NavPress resource published in alliance
with Tyndale House Publishers, Inc.

NAVPRESS

NavPress is the publishing ministry of The Navigators, an international Christian organization and leader in personal spiritual development. NavPress is committed to helping people grow spiritually and enjoy lives of meaning and hope through personal and group resources that are biblically rooted, culturally relevant, and highly practical.

For more information, visit www.NavPress.com.

Printed in the United States of America

22 21 20 19 18 17 16
28 27 26 25 24 23 22

CONTENTS

ACKNOWLEDGMENTS

The LifeChange series has been produced through the coordinated efforts of a team of Navigator Bible study developers and NavPress editorial staff, along with a nationwide network of field-testers.

AUTHOR: WAYNE S. NELSON

SERIES EDITOR: KAREN LEE-THORP

HOW TO USE THIS STUDY

Objectives

Most guides in the LifeChange series of Bible studies cover one book of the Bible. Although the LifeChange guides vary with the books they explore, they share some common goals:

1. To provide you with a firm foundation of understanding and a thirst to return to the book
2. To teach you by example how to study a book of the Bible without structured guides
3. To give you all the historical background, word definitions, and explanatory notes you need, so that your only other reference is the Bible
4. To help you grasp the message of the book as a whole
5. To teach you how to let God's Word transform you into Christ's image

Each lesson in this study is designed to take sixty to ninety minutes to complete on your own. The guide is based on the assumption that you are completing one lesson per week, but if time is limited you can do half a lesson per week or whatever amount allows you to be thorough.

Flexibility

LifeChange guides are flexible, allowing you to adjust the quantity and depth of your study to meet your individual needs. The guide offers many optional questions in addition to the regular numbered questions. The optional questions, which appear in the margins of the study pages, include the following:

Optional Application. Nearly all application questions are optional; we hope you will do as many as you can without overcommitting yourself.

5

For Thought and Discussion. Beginning Bible students should be able to handle these, but even advanced students need to think about them. These questions frequently deal with ethical issues and other biblical principles. They often offer cross-references to spark thought, but the references do not give obvious answers. They are good for group discussions.

For Further Study. These include: (a) cross-references that shed light on a topic the book discusses, and (b) questions that delve deeper into the passage. You can omit them to shorten a lesson without missing a major point of the passage.

If you are meeting in a group, decide together which optional questions to prepare for each lesson, and how much of the lesson you will cover at the next meeting. Normally, the group leader should make this decision, but you might let each member choose his or her own application questions.

As you grow in your walk with God, you will find the LIFECHANGE guide growing with you—a helpful reference on a topic, a continuing challenge for application, a source of questions for many levels of growth.

Overview and details

The study begins with an overview of Exodus. The key to interpretation is context—what is the whole passage or book *about?*—and the key to context is purpose—what is the author's *aim* for the whole work? In lesson 1, you will lay the foundation for your study of Exodus by asking yourself, "Why did the author (and God) write the book? What did they want to accomplish? What is the book about?"

In lessons 2 through 17, you will analyze successive passages of Exodus in detail. Thinking about how a paragraph fits into the overall goal of the book will help you to see its purpose. Its purpose will help you see its meaning. Frequently reviewing a chart or outline of the book will enable you to make these connections.

In lesson 18, you will review Exodus, returning to the big picture to see whether your view of it has changed after closer study. Review will also strengthen your grasp of major issues and give you an idea of how you have grown from your study.

Kinds of questions

Bible study on your own—without a structured guide—follows a progression. First you observe: What does the passage *say?* Then you interpret: What does the passage *mean?* Lastly you apply: How does this truth *affect* my life?

Some of the "how" and "why" questions will take some creative thinking, even prayer, to answer. Some are opinion questions without clear-cut right answers; these will lend themselves to discussions and side studies.

Don't let your study become an exercise in knowledge alone. Treat the passage as God's Word, and stay in dialogue with Him as you study. Pray,

"Lord, what do You want me to see here?" "Father, why is this true?" "Lord, how does this apply to my life?"

It is important that you write down your answers. The act of writing clarifies your thinking and helps you to remember.

Study aids

A list of reference materials, including a few notes of explanation to help you make good use of them, begins on page 163. This guide is designed to include enough background to let you interpret with just your Bible and the guide. Still, if you want more information on a subject or want to study a book on your own, try the references listed.

Scripture versions

Unless otherwise indicated, the Bible quotations in this guide are from the New International Version of the Bible. Other versions cited are the Revised Standard Version (RSV), the New American Standard Bible (NASB), and the King James Version (KJV).

Use any translation you like for study, preferably more than one. A paraphrase such as The Living Bible is not accurate enough for study, but it can be helpful for comparison or devotional reading.

Memorizing and meditating

A psalmist wrote, "I have hidden your word in my heart that I might not sin against you" (Psalm 119:11). If you write down a verse or passage that challenges or encourages you and reflect on it often for a week or more, you will find it beginning to affect your motives and actions. We forget quickly what we read once; we remember what we ponder.

When you find a significant verse or passage, you might copy it onto a card to keep with you. Set aside five minutes during each day just to think about what the passage might mean in your life. Recite it over to yourself, exploring its meaning. Then, return to your passage as often as you can during your day, for a brief review. You will soon find it coming to mind spontaneously.

For group study

A group of four to ten people allows the richest discussions, but you can adapt this guide for other sized groups. It will suit a wide range of group types, such as home Bible studies, growth groups, youth groups, and businessmen's studies. Both new and experienced Bible students, and new and

7

mature Christians, will benefit from the guide. You can omit or leave for later years any questions you find too easy or too hard.

The guide is intended to lead a group through one lesson per week. However, feel free to split lessons if you want to discuss them more thoroughly. Or, omit some questions in a lesson if preparation or discussion time is limited. You can always return to this guide for personal study later. You will be able to discuss only a few questions at length, so choose some for discussion and others for background. Make time at each discussion for members to ask about anything they didn't understand.

Each lesson in the guide ends with a section called "For the Group." These sections give advice on how to focus a discussion, how you might apply the lesson in your group, how you might shorten a lesson, and so on. The group leader should read each "For the group" at least a week ahead so that he or she can tell the group how to prepare for the next lesson.

Each member should prepare for a meeting by writing answers for all of the background and discussion questions to be covered. If the group decides not to take an hour per week for private preparation, then expect to take at least two meetings per lesson to work through the questions. Application will be very difficult, however, without private thought and prayer.

Two reasons for studying in a group are accountability and support. When each member commits in front of the rest to seek growth in an area of life, you can pray with one another, listen jointly for God's guidance, help one another to resist temptation, assure each other that the other's growth matters to you, use the group to practice spiritual principles, and so on. Pray about one another's commitments and needs at most meetings. Spend the first few minutes of each meeting sharing any results from applications prompted by previous lessons. Then discuss new applications toward the end of the meeting. Follow such sharing with prayer for these and other needs.

If you write down each other's applications and prayer requests, you are more likely to remember to pray for them during the week, ask about them at the next meeting, and notice answered prayers. You might want to get a notebook for prayer requests and discussion notes.

Notes taken during discussion will help you to remember, follow up on ideas, stay on the subject, and clarify a total view of an issue. But don't let note-taking keep you from participating. Some groups choose one member at each meeting to take notes. Then someone copies the notes and distributes them at the next meeting. Rotating these tasks can help include people. Some groups have someone take notes on a large pad of paper or erasable marker board so that everyone can see what has been recorded.

Pages 165–166 list some good sources of counsel for leading group studies.

OVERVIEW

To read the Bible with understanding requires that we see both the "forest" and the "trees," the larger context and the small details. We will begin and conclude our study of Exodus by looking at the book as a whole. Once you have a broad grasp of its contents, you will be more able to comprehend its parts. (You may want to just skim some of chapters 25–40.)

First impressions

1. Read Exodus through, at one sitting if possible. Jot answers to question 2 as you read. Use the map to find the places mentioned.

Study Skill — Your Most Important Research Tool

Bible study aids, like this guide, are abundant as never before. We can easily overlook or take for granted what is our most important tool next to a reliable translation of Scripture, for the study of God's Word: an open, inquisitive, and reverent mind.

As you study any portion of the Bible, there is a danger in letting what you have previously thought or heard influence your thinking. It is certainly not necessary to assume that none of your previous knowledge is reliable. However, be careful to let the text speak to you in a fresh way and challenge any misconceptions you have about its meaning. Don't be afraid to ask new questions or even old ones — old questions sometimes cry out for new answers.

Finally, only as you approach the Scriptures with the conviction that they are the Word of God will the Holy Spirit be able to impress their truth upon you. The goal of any study of the Bible should be to know its divine Author and better understand how to glorify Him through your life. May your study of Exodus help you meet these objectives.

---

2. For each of the following portions of the book, list the principle persons, places, and main events or contents.

Chapters 1–4 (persons) _____

_____

(places) _____

_____

(events/contents) _____

_____

_____

Chapters 5–12 (persons) _____

_____

(places) _____

_____

(events/contents) _____

_____

_____

Chapters 13–18 (persons)_____

_____

(places) _____

_____

(events/contents) _____

_____

_____

Chapters 19–24 (persons) _____

_____

(places) _____

_____

(events/contents) _____

_____

_____

Chapters 25–31 (persons) _____

_____

(places) _____

_____

(events/contents) _____

_____

_____

Chapters 32–34 (persons) _____

_____

(places) _____

_____

(events/contents) _____

_____

_____

Chapters 35–40 (persons) _____

_____

(places) _____

_____

(events/contents) _____

_____

_____

3. From this list, what persons, places, events, and themes would you say are the focus of the book?

persons _____

_____

_____

places _____

_____

_____

events _____

_____

_____

themes _____

_____

_____

_____

4. What contrasts do you find between the beginning and end of the book?

_____

_____

_____

5. What characteristics of God does Exodus emphasize?

_____

_____

_____

6. After one reading, how would you summarize the portrait of man (the Egyptians, the Israelites, Moses) that the book presents?

_____

_____

7 Summarize the message of Exodus in one or two sentences. (What is it about? What themes run through it? What seems to be the Holy Spirit's chief aim in giving this book to Israel or the church?)

_____

_____

_____

Now that you've had a chance to form your own impressions of Exodus, here is some background you might find helpful.

The birth of a nation

In the book of Genesis, God began His strategy to restore mankind to intimacy with Him by focusing on a single family: the descendants of Abraham through Isaac and Jacob. Exodus, the next stage of the story, documents four fundamental transformations in this family:

1. Numerical growth, as Israel multiplied from a clan of seventy to a nation of some two million people
2. Geographical movement from Egypt to Sinai
3. Theological development, as Israel exchanged the natural spontaneity of its worship for a structure the Lord Himself revealed
4. Social and spiritual maturation, from human slavery to divine service

As momentous as these changes were, they took place not over decades or years, but within months, weeks, and even hours. In a single night, God not only liberated, but also enriched, His people (see Exodus 12:29-36). Even more, He accomplished all four revolutions in spite of human indifference and opposition.

In recounting Israel's transformation, Exodus never idealizes its characters. It challenges our comfortable theological generalizations. God's people

13

grow suspicious of the very one He used to free them from slavery; they turn to serve idols *after* they have left Egypt far behind. The lines between the "world" and the "church" (to use our terminology) pass, not between nations or groups, but rather through the souls of individual men and women. Not only Pharaoh, but Israel also hardens its heart against the Lord (see Exodus 4:1; 17:1-7; Psalm 95:7-11). Yet at the same time, the Lord defies our modern individualism by dealing with a whole nation as one.

In stark contrast to Israel's conduct, Exodus sets before us Moses. Amidst the confusion, unbelief, and even rebellion of God's people, this man grows to a maturity, authority, and intimacy with God that challenges us to imitate him. In fact, Moses often foreshadows what Christ will be centuries later. He is first God's instrument in delivering Israel, then the mediator between God and Israel. Yet the story does not attempt to hide Moses' failings.

In Exodus, God lays a foundation for Israel's relationship to Him. He reveals His name and its meaning: His character, attributes, and mighty deeds of redemption. He declares His Law that sets the terms of His covenant with Israel under a new administration. Those terms tell how God's people will treat and worship Him, and outline the ethical principles for how a holy people will treat each other. Redemption from slavery, ethics between men, and worship of God are the three great themes of the book, as God explains to Israel, "Who is the Lord, and how shall we relate to Him?" We can break the book into three large sections:

I. Divine Deliverance—Israel created and liberated (1:1–15:21).
II. Divine Decrees—Israel's devotion created and channeled (12:1–13:16; 15:22–24:18).
III. Divine Dwelling—a sanctuary for God's glory in Israel's midst, designed and created (25:1–40:38).

Author and title

Many modern scholars have abandoned the ancient tradition that Moses or someone close to him wrote the bulk of Exodus as a factual historical record. They believe that Exodus is the product of several centuries of experience and reflection, and multiple editings and reelaborations. However, both Exodus and other passages of Scripture say that Moses wrote at least parts of the book (see Exodus 17:14; 24:4; 34:27; Joshua 8:31; Mark 7:10; 12:26; Luke 2:22-23). Furthermore, everywhere in the Old Testament we find references to Moses, the judgments on Egypt, Israel's exodus, and the revelation of the Law through Moses. The Hebrews knew what happened, so we would be foolish to treat Exodus as fiction.[1]

Exodus is a Latin word derived from the Greek word *exodos*, which means "exit" or "departure" (see Luke 9:31; Hebrews 11:22). When the Jews translated the book into Greek around AD 200, they named it *Exodos*. The Hebrew name comes from the book's first two words, *we'elleh shemoth* ("These are the names of"). The same phrase occurs in Genesis 46:8. In both places, it introduces a list of those "who went to Egypt with Jacob" (Exodus 1:1). This repetition shows that Exodus was not meant to be a separate book, but continued a narrative that began in Genesis and extended through Leviticus, Numbers, and Deuteronomy. These five books are known as the Pentateuch ("five-volumed book") or the Torah ("law" or "teaching").

Application

Study Skill — Application

Second Timothy 3:16-17 says "All Scripture . . . is useful for teaching, rebuking, correcting and training in righteousness, so that the servant of God may be thoroughly equipped for every good work." Paul also writes, "For everything that was written in the past was written to teach us, so that through the endurance taught in the Scriptures and the encouragement they provide we might have hope" (Romans 15:4), and "These things happened to them as examples and were written down as warnings for us" (1 Corinthians 10:11). Therefore, when you study Exodus, you should keep asking yourself, "What difference should this passage make in my life? How should it make me want to think or act? How does it encourage, warn, correct, or set me an example?"

Application will require time, thought, prayer, and perhaps even discussion with another person. Sometimes it is more productive to concentrate on one specific application, giving it careful thought and prayer, than to list several potential applications without really reflecting on them or committing yourself to them. At other times, you may want to list many implications that a passage has for your life. Then you can choose one or two of these to act or meditate upon.

---

8. What passages, events, or persons in Exodus seem especially significant to you?

_____

_____

_____

9. In your first reading, did you find any truths that are relevant to your life? If so, was there anything you would like to commit to memory, pray about, or act on? If so, write down your plans.

_____

_____

_____

10. Was there anything in the book that bothered you or that you did not understand? Write your questions here, and plan to pursue answers in one of the books listed in Study Aids, from another Christian whose biblical knowledge you trust, or from your study group.

_____

_____

For the group

This "For the Group" section and the ones in later lessons are intended to suggest ways of structuring your discussions. Feel free to select what suits your group. The main goals of this lesson are to get to know the book of Exodus as a whole and the people with whom you are going to study it. If you have never done a LIFECHANGE study before, you might want to take one meeting to do the "warm-up" below and discuss the "How to Use This Study" section, and a second meeting to discuss lesson 1. This will also give the group more time to read all of Exodus and answer the questions in lesson 1.

Worship. Some groups like to begin with prayer and/or singing. Some share requests for prayer at the beginning but leave the actual prayer until after the study. Others prefer just to chat and have refreshments for a while, then open the study with a brief prayer for the Holy Spirit's guidance, and leave worship and prayer until the end.

Warm-up. The beginning of a new study is a good time to lay a foundation for honest sharing of ideas, to get comfortable with each other, and to encourage a sense of common purpose. One way to establish common ground is to talk about what each person hopes to get out of your study of Exodus, and out of any prayer, singing, sharing, outreach, or anything else you might do together. You can also share what you hope to give as well as get. If you have someone write down each member's hopes and expectations then you can look back at these goals later to see if they are being met. Goal setting at the beginning can also help you avoid confusion when one person thinks the main point of the group is to learn the Scripture, while another thinks it is to support each other in daily Christian life, and another thinks prayer or outreach is the chief business.

How to Use This Study. Advise group members to read the "How to Use This Study" section if they have not already done so. You might go over important points that you think the group should especially notice. For example, point out the optional questions in the margins. These are available as group discussion questions, ideas for application, and suggestions for further study. It is unlikely that anyone will have the time or desire to answer all the optional questions and do all the applications. A person might do one "Optional Application" for any given lesson. You might choose one or two "For Thought and Discussion" questions for your group discussion, or you might spend all your time on the numbered questions. If someone wants to write answers to the optional questions, suggest that he use a separate notebook. It will also be helpful for discussion notes, prayer requests, answers to prayers, application plans, and so on. Invite everyone to ask questions about the "How to Use This Study" section.

Overview. Ideally, everyone should have read the whole book of Exodus and the background before you meet together. However, some may not have done so, and others may not retain much of what they read quickly. Encourage any group members who found the overview to be a lot of work; it is by far the most time-consuming lesson of the study.

Begin by asking for everyone's overall impressions of Exodus. Did you enjoy the book? Was it dull or exciting? Which parts did you find the most fun or the most edifying? Which parts seemed to be less relevant to your lives?

You might use a chalkboard to jot the group's answers to question 2. Circle people, places, events, and themes that seem most important in tying the book together (question 3). Then discuss questions 4 through 7.

Next, ask someone to tell briefly how the story of Exodus relates to what happens in Genesis. Then, have someone else quickly link Exodus to what happens in the rest of the Old Testament. Finally, what does Exodus have to do with the events of the New Testament? If the group has trouble with any of these questions, a Bible handbook, commentary on Exodus, or Old Testament survey will give answers. Ask a group member or the leader to come next time with this information.

Let everyone share questions he or she has about the book. Save these to answer as you study in detail, and come back to them at the end to see if you have answered all of them.

Don't spend a lot of time on application in this lesson. Later lessons will attempt to guide those who are unsure how to apply Scripture to their lives. However, do share any ways you were able to identify with the characters and incidents in the story, and any ways you found the book relevant to your lives. Questions 9 and 10 should help you get to know each other better and give everyone something to think about during the week.

Wrap-up. Briefly tell the group what to expect in lesson 2. Whet everyone's appetite, and ask the group to think about any optional questions that you plan to discuss.

Worship. Many groups like to end with singing and/or prayer. This can include songs or prayers that respond to what you've learned in Bible study or prayers for specific needs of group members. Some people are shy about sharing personal needs or praying aloud in groups, especially before they know the other people well. If this is true of your group, then a song and/or some silent prayer and a short closing prayer spoken by the leader might be an appropriate ending.

1. For a detailed discussion of authorship and date of composition, see any of the commentaries on page 163, or see W. S. LaSor, D. A. Hubbard, and F. W. Bush, *Old Testament Survey* (Grand Rapids, MI: Eerdmans, 1982).

From Egypt to Sinai

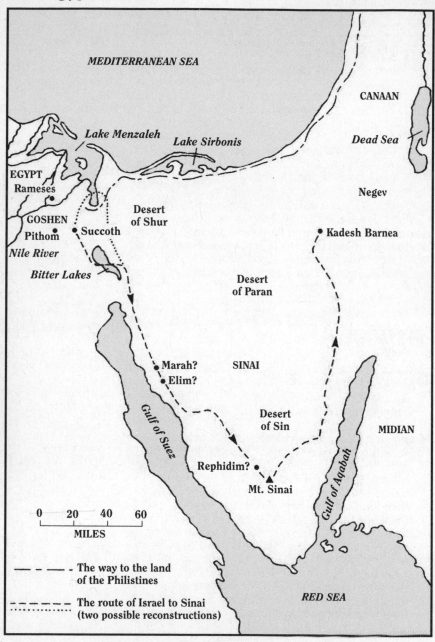

MEDITERRANEAN SEA

CANAAN

Lake Menzaleh

Lake Sirbonis

Dead Sea

EGYPT
Rameses

Negev

Desert
of Shur

GOSHEN
Pithom
Succoth

Kadesh Barnea

Nile River

Bitter Lakes

Desert
of Paran

Marah?
Elim?

SINAI

Desert
of Sin

MIDIAN

Gulf of Suez

Gulf of Aqabah

Rephidim?

Mt. Sinai

0   20   40   60
MILES

— — — — The way to the land
of the Philistines

— — — — — The route of Israel to Sinai
········· (two possible reconstructions)

RED SEA

EXODUS 1:1–2:25

Birth Pains

Genesis opens with the creation of the world and mankind. Exodus begins with the birth of the nation Israel, and of one child who will lead that nation to its spiritual birth as the people of God. Read 1:1–2:25 before beginning the questions in this lesson. Sense the mood of the story at this point.

Oppression (1:1-22)

Israel (1:1). God renamed Jacob "Israel" (Genesis 32:28; 35:10). The descendants of Jacob/Israel came to be called by his name.

Joseph (1:5-8). Jacob's eleventh son. His brothers sold him into slavery, but he became the Prime Minister of Egypt. When famine struck the whole region, Jacob sent his other sons from Canaan to Egypt to buy grain. There they met their long-lost brother, who at first terrified them but then revealed that he had forgiven their treachery. As the famine worsened, Joseph persuaded his brothers and father to join him in Egypt. Since Joseph was the current king's right-hand man, his family was welcomed (see Genesis 38–50). However, after some two hundred years, the Egyptian kings forgot what Joseph had done for the country and began to

For Thought and Discussion: In what sense did the new king not "know" Joseph (1:8)?

For Thought and Discussion: God fulfilled His promise of fruitfulness even under Egyptian oppression. What does this say about Him?

Optional Application: Does your situation look as bleak as Israel's? What signs do you already see that God has heard your cries, has remembered His commitment to you, and is already sowing the seeds of your deliverance? Ask Him to open your eyes to these signs of hope.

view the descendants of Jacob as an inferior and dangerous minority.

1. "The Israelites were exceedingly fruitful; they multiplied greatly" and filled the land (Exodus 1:7). This fact is so important to this chapter that it is mentioned three times (see 1:7,12,20). To whom had God promised this would happen?

Genesis 1:28 _____

Genesis 9:1 _____

Genesis 17:2,6; 22:17 _____

Genesis 26:4 _____

Genesis 28:14; 35:11; 48:4 _____

2. What is the point here? What link do these passages suggest?

_____

_____

_____

_____

Pharaoh (1:11). This meant "great house" in Egyptian. It was a royal title, not the king's personal name.[1]

3. What "shrewd" strategies did Pharaoh decree in his attempt to control the growth of the Hebrew population (see 1:11-14)?

_____

_____

_____

_____

4. What were the results of these measures (see 1:15-22)?

20

_____

_____

_____

_____

_____

5. How did God feel about His people's sufferings (see 2:23-25)?

_____

_____

_____

_____

6. Why do you think He allowed His people to suffer under the Egyptians?

_____

_____

_____

_____

7. The Hebrew "midwives feared God" (1:21). How did their actions show it?

_____

_____

_____

_____

8. What does it mean to "fear God" in a good sense? (Consider Exodus 1:15-21; Luke 12:4-12.)

_____

_____

Optional Application: What social pressures — perhaps more subtle but just as real as the pressures on the midwives — are on you to do wrong? How can a fear of the Lord help you resist them?

For Thought and Discussion: Against the backdrop of national events, we learn about one individual, Moses. Why do you think this balance between the many and the one is so frequent and important in the Bible?

For Further Study:
What similarities and differences do you find between Exodus 2 and Matthew 2? Why did Jesus relive Israel's history leading toward the Exodus?

For Thought and Discussion: What role do women play in 1:1–2:10? What might be the point of the repeated mention of women's actions versus Pharaoh's intentions?

Optional Application:
a. Moses' attempt to help his people involved violence and ended in failure. How can you avoid letting your emotions draw you into unwise actions?
b. If a current injustice seems to be crying out for redress, take time daily this week to pray earnestly for the Lord to reveal wise and good means of bringing justice.

_____

_____

Moses (2:1-25)

___

Moses (2:10). "The name, of Egyptian origin, means 'is born' and forms the second element in such pharaonic names as Ahmose . . . Thutmose and Rameses."[2] *Drew him out* is a Hebrew wordplay on the name, since "Moses" sounds like the Hebrew for "draw out." The pun refers not only to Moses' deliverance from the Nile, but also prophetically to what God would do at the Red Sea.

___

9. Summarize the important events of Moses' infancy (see 1:22–2:10).

_____

_____

_____

_____

_____

10. What is ironic about 1:22–2:10?

_____

_____

_____

11. How did Moses try to demonstrate his commitment to his own people (see 2:11-14)?

_____

_____

_____

_____

_____

For Thought and Discussion: What spiritual contrasts do you sense between the Israelites in chapter 1 and in chapter 2?

Moses had grown up (2:11). He was now forty years old (see Acts 7:23).

Midian (2:15). The Midianites probably descended from one of Abraham's younger sons (see Genesis 25:2). They lived in southeastern Sinai and west central Arabia, on either side of the Gulf of Aqaba (an arm of the Red Sea). This parched semi-desert and its tribes of wandering shepherds were a sharp change for a man raised in the luxurious Egyptian court. Moses wandered with the tribe's flocks in Midian for forty years (see Acts 7:29-30).

Priest of Midian (2:16). His personal name was Reuel ("friend of God"), and his title was Jethro (which probably meant "his excellency") —2:18; 3:1.[3]

For Thought and Discussion:
   a. Put yourself in Moses' place. How would you feel living as an Egyptian nobleman, knowing that the Egyptians were oppressing your own family?
   b. How would you feel if you were suddenly thrust out of your comfortable, familiar home and into a desolate land to keep sheep and sleep in tents with strangers?

12. What do you learn about Moses' character at this stage of his life from . . .

    2:11-14? _____

    _____

    _____

    2:15-22? _____

    _____

    _____

13. What is ironic about the question in 2:14? (Consider: Who did make Moses ruler and judge over Israel?)

    _____

    _____

    _____

23

For Further Study:
To better understand
the covenant and
God's blessings on
Israel, read Genesis
12:1-20.

14. God "heard" and "remembered" Israel (2:24). How has He shown His concern for Israel already in these first two chapters?

_____

_____

_____

_____

_____

Covenant (2:24). One of the most important words in the Old Testament. It is used for treaties and alliances between nations or peoples (see 1 Samuel 11:1), agreements between individuals (see Genesis 21:27), friendship pacts (see 1 Samuel 18:3-4), and most importantly, the relationship between God and humans (see Genesis 6:18; 15:18; 17:4-14). In all of these uses, intimate, personal knowledge, responsibilities, and privileges are implied. A covenant could be between equals, but it need not be. The Lord chose Abraham and his descendants through Isaac and Jacob as His people by a free act of His grace, independent of any merit on their part (see Deuteronomy 7:7-11).[4] The covenant between God and Israel is most like a treaty between a sovereign and a subject people — a common thing in the ancient Near East. It is also like a marriage contract (see God's jealousy in Exodus 20:5).

Your response

15. What insight from 1:1–2:25 seems most personally significant to you right now? (This might be an example worth following or avoiding, a truth about God, and so on.)

_____

_____

_____

_____

_____

16. How would you like this insight to affect you—
    your character, habits, priorities, attitudes?

    _____

    _____

    _____

    _____

17. How can you begin putting this into practice
    this week? (What decision should you make,
    what persistent prayer can you offer, what active
    steps can you take?)

    _____

    _____

    _____

    _____

18. If you have any questions about 1:1–2:25 or
    anything in this lesson, write them down.

    _____

    _____

    _____

    _____

For the group

Warm-up. People often come to Bible study groups
with their minds still full of the day's busyness.

Beginning with worship can help people change mental gears to focus on God. One way to help them open up to each other and start thinking about the issues you are going to discuss is to ask a question about their lives that relates to the topic at hand. In this lesson, you might ask, "Have you ever cried out to God and felt as though He wasn't hearing or didn't care because nothing seemed to be happening?" Encourage anyone to describe briefly such an experience, but give everyone the freedom to pass.

Read aloud. It is usually helpful to have someone read the whole passage aloud before you start discussing it. This refreshes everyone's memory, sets the tone of the discussion, and may even let people notice details they hadn't seen before. With long narrative passages as in Exodus, it can be fun to assign the parts of the narrator and the various characters to different readers. Ask each to read with the tone of voice he or she thinks Pharaoh, the midwives, and others would have used.

Summarize. Before you dive into the details, ask someone to summarize what happens in 1:1–2:25.

Questions. It is not necessary to discuss each question in equal detail, especially if the group has prepared answers at home. You might skip some simple observations entirely and cover others quickly with one or two responses. Or, you might omit a whole section of questions in order to focus on some aspect that seems especially relevant or interesting to the group. Even if you spend most of your time on one or two "For Thought and Discussion" questions and get something out of them, you have used your time well.

Try to allow at least fifteen minutes to discuss how what you have studied applies to you. Encourage each person to come away from the meeting committed to some action. This might be a decision to pray for God's intervention in some situation with greater trust in His love and timing. It might be a commitment to imitate the midwives by refusing to go along with some moral pressure (to bend the truth, to put money or success ahead of your family or the Lord). It might be a decision to pray daily about some injustice that is bothering you instead of lashing out. It might even be a

26

conviction that you need to take some action on that injustice, while praying to avoid self-righteous anger. Help group members get specific about their plans for application.

There may be times when someone finds nothing in a passage that seems important to apply immediately. The big issue he needs to act on now may be dealt with somewhere else in Scripture, or he may still want to focus on his application from the last lesson. This is fine. If a group member can't find anything in 1:1–2:25 to apply, ask him or her to share what issue God is working on in his or her life now, and what he or she is doing about it.

Summarize. Before you close, ask someone to summarize your discussion briefly. What major lessons did you learn about God, His people, and yourselves? What are some of the ways group members plan to act on what they have learned?

Prayer. Take time to pray together about each of your applications. If someone has committed himself to pray about some personal need or an injustice that is bothering him, pray together about that. If someone has decided to take action or resist sin in some area, pray for that person. Ask the Lord to hear your cries and remember you as He did Israel, and to act in your lives as supernaturally as He did in the lives of Moses and his people.

Egypt

The region around the Nile River, in the northeast corner of Africa, supported what may be the world's oldest civilization. Over three thousand years before Christ, Upper (southern) and Lower (northern) Egypt were united under a single monarch. The great pyramids were constructed over a thousand years before Moses' birth. The Egyptians made advances in architecture, agriculture, and medicine. They were skilled in the practical application of mathematics, though their ability to formulate mathematical principles was limited. They also developed a sophisticated linguistic system that used several different kinds of writing. Finally, they were careful observers of the heavens and had an accurate calendar that

(continued on page 28)

(continued from page 27)

distinguished between calendar and solar years. Politically, Egypt was Canaan's overlord while Israel was forming in Egypt.

Despite their four hundred years in Egypt, the Hebrews seem to have been little influenced by Egyptian culture. This was particularly true in religious and spiritual matters. Israel's monotheism was in sharp contrast to Egyptian polytheism (worship of many gods) and the Levitical priesthood's purpose and function was far different from that of Egypt. Finally, Israel's and Egypt's perspectives on death and the after-life had almost nothing in common; the Old Testament reveals little on this subject, but the Egyptians are famous for the elaborate preparations they made for life after death, and their religious literature is much occupied with this subject. Yet though Israel was not affected culturally by Egypt, it never forgot that it had been enslaved there and found liberation and life only through God's intervention.[5]

1. Kenneth Barker, ed., *The NIV Study Bible* (Grand Rapids, MI: Zondervan, 1985), 88.
2. Barker, 89.
3. Barker, 89.
4. Elmer B. Smick, "Covenant," *Theological Wordbook of the Old Testament,* vol. 1, ed. R. L. Harris, et. al. (Chicago: Moody, 1980), 128–130.
5. For more information on Egypt, see the article in *The New Bible Dictionary,* 2nd ed., ed. J. D. Douglas, et. al. (Wheaton, IL: Tyndale, 1982), 301–310; or "Egypt" in *The International Standard Bible Encyclopedia,* rev. ed., vol. 2, ed. Geoffrey W. Bromiley (Grand Rapids, MI: Eerdmans, 1982), 29–47.

EXODUS 3:1–4:31

Whom God Called, and Why

Aware of His people's sufferings, God was ready to intervene. He had chosen a man to be the catalyst for their liberation. But there were problems. That man was unaware of God's plan, and when he learned about it, he wanted no part of it. Read 3:1–4:31, and try to put yourself in Moses' place.

1. Basically, what happens in 3:1–4:31?

_____

_____

_____

2. What was it about the burning bush that first attracted Moses' attention (see 3:1-3)?

_____

_____

3. How did Moses react upon learning he was in the presence of God (see 3:4-6)? Why did he react this way?

_____

_____

_____

For Further Study: Compare Moses' call to other calls in 1 Samuel 3:1-21; 9:27–10:8; Isaiah 6:1-13; Jeremiah 1:4-19; Ezekiel 1:1–3:11; Matthew 4:18-22; Acts 9:1-9.

The angel of the LORD (3:2). The Bible contains
dozens of references to this person. Both the
Hebrew and Greek terms could be translated
as either "messenger" or "angel." It is usually
clear that a supernatural being is meant. The
figure is "a heavenly being sent by God to deal
with man as his personal agent and spokes-
man. In many passages he is virtually identified with God and speaks not merely in the
name of God but as God in the first person sin-
gular."[1] (Notice that Exodus 3:4 says it was God
Himself in the bush. Likewise Genesis 16:7-11
speaks of the angel of the Lord, but Genesis
16:13 says Hagar saw the Lord Himself.)
   Many have seen the angel of the Lord as
an appearance of Christ before His incarnation.
However, the New Testament does not say this,
and the angel of the Lord in the New Testament
is definitely not God the Son (see Matthew
1:20,24; 2:13; Luke 2:9; Acts 5:19). One writer
states: "It is certain that from the beginning
God used angels in human form, with human
voices, in order to communicate with man, and
the appearances of the angel of the Lord, with
his special redemptive relation to God's people,
show the working of that divine mode of self-
revelation which culminated in the coming of
the Savior, and are thus a foreshadowing of,
and a preparation for, the full revelation of God
in Jesus Christ. Further than this it is not safe
to go."[2]

Fire (3:2). "God's revelation of himself and his will
was often accompanied by fire"[3] (see Exodus
13:21; 19:18; 1 Kings 18:24,38).

Holy (3:5). Set apart from the commonplace. The
ancients recognized two categories of things.
On one hand were common things, humans,
and animals. On the other side of a chasm were
holy beings and everything that belonged to
them. Most people thought of holy in terms of
power, strangeness, and inscrutability. All the
"divine" beings were holy, from the least tree
spirit to the father of the gods. Holiness did not
imply morality or love at all.
   Therefore, one of God's chief tasks in
training Israel was to change the nation's

idea of holiness. First, He stressed that only He was holy, not the gods and spirits of the pagans. Second, what belonged to Him was untouchably, radically holy and was set apart in dramatic ceremonies to emphasize its separation from the commonplace. Third, because morality (righteousness) was an essential trait of the Holy Lord, it was an essential trait of holiness. Anyone unrighteous was therefore unholy and could not approach the Holy God. Everyone set apart for the Lord had to be righteous or face His wrath. As you study Exodus, you will see how God begins to instill these truths.

Optional Application:
a. Do you think 2:14-15 may have made Moses reluctant to respond to God's call? Why or why not?
b. Do you use your past failures as excuses for not doing what God has commanded? If so, ask God to help you stop doing this, and decide for yourself to resist this temptation and obey.

For Thought and Discussion: a. Could Moses have accepted the answer in 3:12 without exercising faith in this God? Why or why not?
b. What are the implications for you?

4. The Lord revealed what He intended to do about Israel's suffering, and Moses' part in the plan (see 3:7-10). What five objections did Moses raise?

3:11 _____

_____

3:13 _____

_____

4:1 _____

_____

4:10 _____

_____

4:13 _____

_____

5. How did God respond to the false humility of "Who am I? [I'm nobody]" (3:11-12)?

_____

_____

_____

_____

31

6. How did God deal with Moses' second objection (see 3:13-22)?

_____

_____

_____

_____

_____

Name (3:13,15). In ancient times, someone's name expressed his character, his identity. Although the Lord's name was in use before now (it is found throughout Genesis), He now begins to reveal what that name means through what He does (see Exodus 6:3; 15:3; 33:18-19; 34:5-7).

I AM WHO I AM (3:14). Most commentators agree that in Hebrew, the emphasis in "I AM" is not on God's abstract existence but on His active presence. "Specifically, the stress is upon God's presence with Moses and Israel, his 'being' is a 'being with', a divine presence."[4] "I am" in 3:14 is the same Hebrew word as "I will be" in "I will be *with you*" (3:12). J. P. Hyatt suggests the translation "I will be what I will be" in the sense that God "will disclose his name and nature to Moses and Israel as he is active in their life and history."[5]

The LORD (3:15). The Hebrew is *YHWH*. It means "He is" or "He will be"; it is the third person form of the verb rendered "I will be" in 3:12 and "I AM" in 3:14. (When God speaks of Himself, He says "I AM." When we speak of Him, we say "He is.")

Because of 20:7, the Jews later decided that God's name was too holy to use at all. So they said *Adonai* ("my Lord") whenever the Bible said *YHWH*. The true pronunciation of the name has thus been forgotten, but modern scholars think it is "Yahweh." Some versions use "Jehovah," an older guess, and other translations use "the LORD."

7. In 3:14-22, the Lord elaborates on the basic plan in 3:7-10. What new elements does He add?

_____

_____

_____

_____

_____

Flowing with milk and honey (3:8,17). Egypt receives almost no rainfall, and its only arable land is the four percent that surrounds the Nile. Canaan was very different. It lay on the western tip of the Fertile Crescent and while it was not uniformly lush, it received enough rain and had enough streams and springs to permit the cultivation of many crops and the raising of livestock.

8. In his third objection (see 4:1), Moses attributes unbelief to Israel. To what extent do you think this was fair, and to what extent does it just show Moses' lack of faith? (Is 4:31 relevant?)

_____

_____

_____

_____

9. How did God disarm this third objection (see 4:2-9)?

_____

_____

_____

_____

_____

Optional Application: What excuses are you making for not doing what God has called you to do? Has He provided the resources — both within you and from others — that you need? Pray about this. Ask for the resources, and for the faith to trust God in this task.

33

For Further Study:
How is Moses' objection that he is not eloquent answered by
1 Corinthians 1:17–2:5 and 1 Thessalonians 5:1?

For Thought and Discussion: Why do you think God made the concession in 4:14-17? What does this say about His character?

Optional Application: While Israel was suffering, Moses was stalling. Is your unwillingness to obey the Lord prolonging the problems other Christians are facing? Pray, and make some decisions.

10. How would you paraphrase (put into your own words) the Lord's response to the fourth excuse (see 4:11-12)?

_____

_____

_____

_____

11. Even though God refused to let Moses "off the hook," He did make a concession to him. What was it (see 4:14-17)?

_____

_____

_____

_____

12. If nothing else, Moses' excuses gave the Lord a chance to reveal Himself and His character. What does 3:1–4:17 reveal about . . .

God? _____

_____

_____

_____

_____

Moses at this stage of his life? _____

_____

_____

_____

Lᴏʀᴅ *was about to kill him* (4:24-26). This strange incident has puzzled many readers. God had commanded that all of Abraham's male descendants be circumcised (see Genesis 17:9-14) as

34

a sign of "cutting" the covenant and offering themselves wholly to God. The rite invited God to "cut off" the man from the nation if he broke the covenant. However, the Egyptians found circumcision disgusting, so Moses may not have been circumcised as a child. Moses' wife performed the rite on their son and with the severed foreskin touched Moses' "feet." (The Hebrew word for *feet* may be a polite substitute for the sexual organs, as in Deuteronomy 28:57.) In that way, his child's circumcision would count for him as well.[6] The other possible interpretation is that Moses had not bothered to circumcise his son, and God held him responsible for the neglect.[7]

13. What further information do we get about God's plans in 4:18-23?

_____

_____

_____

14. How would you state the main point or theme of 3:1–4:31?

_____

_____

_____

_____

Your response

15. What one aspect of 3:1–4:31 would you like to take to heart?

_____

_____

_____

_____

Optional Application: Exodus 4:11-17 suggests that "God will not work without us, but He will send someone else with us." Is this true in your life? If so, how is it encouraging you to act?

Optional Application: Are you focused on the problems in your situation to the extent that you feel helpless? Or, are you fixed on God's power to overcome them? Specifically, what should you do?

For Thought and Discussion: Put yourself in Aaron's place. You have not been raised with your brother and have not seen him for years. How would you react to a message from the Lord as in 4:27? What do you learn about Aaron from this?

For Further Study:
What does 3:1–4:17 suggest about man's ability to refuse God or frustrate His purposes?

16. How do you fall short or need to grow in this area?

_____

_____

_____

_____

_____

17. What steps can you take to move forward in this process this week? What active application can you make?

_____

_____

_____

_____

_____

18. List any questions you have about 3:1–4:31.

_____

_____

_____

_____

For the group

Warm-up. Ask, "Think of some situation that is currently worrying, frustrating, or concerning you. What seems to be the biggest thing that keeps you from effectively doing something about it?"

Read aloud. Ask three group members to read the parts of the narrator, God, and Moses with appropriate tones of voice. This can be a fun dialogue if done well.

Questions. As you identify each of Moses' objections and how God deals with it, discuss how any of you have made similar excuses for not doing what God has said. Encourage group members to be open about their experiences. What instructions from God is each of you wrestling with? How can you help one another take these possibly scary steps?

Prayer. Ask God to help each of you fulfill the plans He has for you. Ask Him to override all your excuses and provide all the resources you need. Ask Him for the confidence that although you may not feel competent, He will be with you. Pray for the assurance of His character, and for the confidence that He is able to convince people. Ask for, and expect, help from other people.

Israel in Egypt

God called Abraham to leave his home in Mesopotamia (modern Iraq) for a land that his descendants would receive as their own. Why, then, did God multiply Israel into a nation of two million in Egypt rather than Canaan? There seem to be at least five reasons:

First, it was necessary that Israel be formed as a nation in circumstances that kept her distinct and unique. In Canaan, Jacob's family was almost absorbed by the existing population (see Genesis 34). In Egypt, on the other hand, Israel never risked assimilation; the Egyptians took care to segregate the Hebrews because they scorned shepherds (see Genesis 46:28–47:6).

Second, in Egypt, God preserved Israel from the moral corruption that was so rife in Canaan. While the Egyptians were pagans, their religious and social practices were not as debauched (the Canaanites practiced child sacrifice and ritual prostitution).

Third, Israel would be God's instrument of judgment against the wicked Canaanites. God was waiting until "the sin of the Amorites [the Canaanites] . . . reached its full measure" (Genesis 15:16). Then He would bring His people in to annihilate them.

Fourth, Israel had to learn to trust God rather than men. As long as there was a pharaoh who remembered Joseph, the Hebrews were treated with respect. But when a pharaoh

(continued on page 38)

(continued from page 37)
arose who did not "know" Joseph, they fell quickly from favor. Clearly, dependence on God rather than political alliances was the only way for Israel to survive.

Finally, God desired to birth Israel in circumstances that would display His power and glory. As Israel multiplied even under oppression, it became evident to everyone that God's blessing was upon His people.

1. J. B. Taylor, "Angel of the Lord," *The New Bible Dictionary*, 2nd ed., ed. J. D. Douglas, et. al. (Wheaton, IL: Tyndale, 1982), 38.
2. J. M. Wilson, "Angel," *The International Standard Bible Encyclopedia*, vol. 1 (Grand Rapids, MI: Eerdmans, 1982), 125.
3. Kenneth Barker, ed., *The NIV Study Bible* (Grand Rapids, MI: Zondervan, 1985), 90.
4. J. P. Hyatt, *Exodus* (London: Oliphants, 1971), 76.
5. Hyatt, 76.
6. John I. Durham, *Exodus* (Waco, TX: Word, 1987), 56–59; William Gispen, *Exodus* (Grand Rapids, MI: Zondervan, 1982), 63–64.
7. Gispen, 63–64.

EXODUS 5:1–6:27

The Word and Name of the Lord

Moses did his best to get out of what God told him to do; he just had this nagging feeling that something would go wrong. Either Israel wouldn't believe him or he would louse it up. To his astonishment, the Hebrews did believe him and sent him and Aaron off to see Pharaoh. But just as Moses was starting to have reasons to relax and pat himself on the back, his worst fears proved true. Read 5:1–6:27, putting yourself in the shoes of Moses and the Israelites.

Bricks without straw (5:1-18)

This is what the LORD . . . says (5:1). "Thus saith the LORD" in KJV. This phrase occurs here for the first time in Scripture. It is the hallmark of the prophet. It declares that not only does God reveal His will to people so that they might know and obey Him, but He reveals it through other people. Moses and Aaron are God's authorized spokesmen to Pharaoh, His messengers, His ambassadors. Pharaoh's response to them constitutes his response to God (see 7:1).

"Thus says the Lord" or its equivalent is on the lips of prophets throughout the Old Testament. Because it implies a serious claim, its abuse is severely punished (see Exodus 20:7; 1 Kings 22:13-28; Jeremiah 28:1-17). God sends prophets to call Israel back to Himself, and

For Thought and Discussion: Pharaoh looked at religious sacrifice as an idle distraction from work (see 5:17). How does this resemble modern secular thought?

He sends them to the pagan nations as well. Moses' confrontation with Pharaoh foreshadows the emphasis of the later prophets on God's rule over all the earth.

1. What is Pharaoh's opinion of the sincerity of Moses and Aaron's request (see 5:4-5)?

2. How does Pharaoh deal with this irritation (see 5:6-9)?

3. The Lord's message is "Let my people go" (5:1). What challenge to Pharaoh's authority does this imply?

4. In complaining to Pharaoh, the Israelite foremen refer to themselves as "your servants" (5:15-16). Do the foremen look at things the way the Lord does? Explain.

God's reassurance (5:19–6:27)

5. What accusations do the foremen level at Moses and Aaron (see 5:19-21)? Explain in your own words.

_____

_____

_____

_____

_____

6. To what degree is this accusation accurate?

_____

_____

_____

_____

7. Of what does Moses then accuse God (see 5:22-23)?

_____

_____

_____

_____

8. How does the Lord deal with Moses' complaint (see 6:1)?

_____

_____

_____

_____

_____

For Thought and Discussion: What does 5:21 have in common with 2:14? What would you do if you kept hearing things like this?

Optional Application:
a. How frank is Moses with God about his thoughts and feelings in 5:22-23?
b. Are you this honest with God? How can you put Moses' example into practice?

41

For Thought and Discussion: In 3:1–4:31, we saw Moses confronted by the reality of God. In 5:1–6:12, we see him face the reality of human opposition and unbelief. How did all this contribute to Moses' growth as a disciple and a leader?

Optional Application: For Moses, serving God meant involvement with suffering people, but not instant remedies. Is your presence with and commitment to those in need a tangible proof of God's compassion? Think of some person or group with whom you can get involved and demonstrate God's grace.

9. He goes on to elaborate what He has already declared in 3:1-22. What is new or especially important in 6:2-8?

_____

_____

_____

_____

_____

God Almighty (6:3). *El Shaddai* means "God, the Almighty One."

By my name the LORD I did not make myself fully known (6:3). The name is used often in Genesis. Also, "Jochebed" in Exodus 6:20 means "*YHWH* is glory." So, the Lord is not saying that the patriarchs were utterly ignorant of His name. Rather, they did not understand its implications of faithful presence. In delivering Israel and fulfilling His promises, the Lord is about to let His people *know* (intimately and by experience) His name.

10. God repeats "I am the LORD" four times in 6:2-8. Why do you think He does this? (Recall 3:13-15; 5:2; 6:3.)

_____

_____

_____

_____

Redeem (6:6). To attain ownership or release of something or someone by paying a price.

11. Notice the verbs in 6:6-8 ("I will bring . . . I will free . . . I will redeem . . . I will take . . . I will be your God . . . I will give"). What do these phrases tell you about the meaning of the Lord's name?

_____

_____

_____

_____

_____

12. Why do you think the Lord allowed things to get worse for Israel? (Consider 3:19-20; 6:1,6-8.)

_____

_____

_____

_____

13. How does Israel's response to the new revelation from God (see 6:9) compare with the people's previous one (see 4:31)?

_____

_____

_____

_____

14. Do you think this is justifiable? Why or why not?

_____

_____

_____

_____

_____

Optional Application: How has God brought you out of slavery, freed you, redeemed you, taken you as His own, and become your God? Take time to thank Him for doing this. How can you live this week in light of the fact that you have been redeemed and now belong to God?

For Further Study: Moses says he is "uncircumcised of lips" (Exodus 6:12, NIV margin). "(Un)circumcised" occurs in a figurative sense also in Leviticus 19:23; 26:41; Deuteronomy 10:16; 30:6; Jeremiah 4:4; 6:10; 9:26. What does it mean in each passage?

For Thought and Discussion: It often seems that things have to get worse before they get better. Why do you think this is so?

Optional Application: Would you react as Israel did (see 5:19-21; 6:9) if God didn't fix your situation fast enough? Are you even now angry and discouraged? If so, ask God to enable you to trust His love, power, and timing. Meditate on 6:2 this week.

For Thought and Discussion: Why do you think the author inserts a genealogy of Moses and Aaron in 4:13-27?

Your response

15. What aspect of 5:1–6:27 seems most personally significant to you?

_____

_____

_____

_____

_____

16. How would you like this to affect your life?

_____

_____

_____

_____

_____

_____

17. What action can you take this week in light of this truth?

_____

_____

_____

_____

18. Write down any questions you have about 5:1–6:27.

_____

_____

_____

_____

For the group

Warm-up. Ask group members to share their current moods and feelings about something for which they are deeply concerned. You don't want to be tyrannized by your feelings, but being honest about your feelings will help you know each other, God, and yourselves better. Plan to pray about your feelings at the end of your meeting.

Read aloud and summarize.

Questions. This whole episode is largely a lesson about trusting God and knowing His character even when things seem to be getting worse instead of better. You may feel you want to apply it to some unpleasant situation you are now facing. On the other hand, the Christian's exodus from enslavement to sin and death has already been accomplished. Especially if some of you are facing hard times, ask the group how God has revealed Himself to each of you as the One who is actively present with you, the One who has already brought you out, freed you, redeemed you, and taken you as His own. Focus with gratitude on your already finished exodus, so that you will be better able to trust God for that part that is not yet complete. How are you now experiencing God's active presence in your lives?

Prayer. Thank God for already redeeming you, and for the ways you even now experience His active presence with you. Confess your feelings about your circumstances, and ask God to give you peaceful trust in His ability to handle them. Worship Him as the Lord who is.

When Was the Exodus?

The date of the exodus is hotly debated. The evidence includes other passages of Scripture that give chronological information, references in Exodus itself, other ancient nations' records, and archaeological remains. The two most popular dates are:

1. Around 1446 BC. The exodus from Egypt took place 480 years before "the fourth year

(continued on page 46)

(continued from page 45)

of Solomon's reign over Israel" according to 1 Kings 6:1, and Solomon's reign definitely started in 970 BC. This date also fits with Judges 11:26. Also, recent research suggests that two of the pharaohs of Egypt's eighteenth dynasty, Thutmose III and his son Amenhotep II, were the kind of men who would have enslaved a whole people in order to build cities.

2. Around 1290 BC. Exodus 1:11 names the city as "Rameses," which suggests that the oppressing pharaohs were Seti I and his son Rameses II of the nineteenth dynasty. Archaeologists think that the evidence of many cities destroyed in Canaan in the 1200s BC suggests that Joshua's invasion took place then. However, "Rameses" in Exodus 1:11 and Genesis 47:11 may well have been editorial updates by someone generations after Moses, and the archaeological evidence is disputed. The dating question may never be settled, but fortunately it does not interfere with an understanding of the text.

EXODUS 6:28–10:29

Judgments on Egypt: 1

As the Lord expected, Pharaoh is not about to listen to some desert shepherd claiming to be a prophet of some tribal god. Since Pharaoh says he doesn't know the Lord well enough to obey Him (see 5:2), the Lord will see to it that he gets to know the God of Israel better. Read 6:28–10:29, looking for repeated elements that suggest a pattern. You might want to jot down your answers to questions 3 and 4 as you read.

1. What does God reveal to Moses about the process by which He will liberate Israel (see 7:1-5)?

_____

_____

_____

_____

For Thought and Discussion: What gave Moses the courage to confront Egypt's ruler? What does his example teach you about the attitude you should have toward God and people, whatever their social standing?

Snake (7:9). "Throughout much of Egypt's history the pharaoh wore a cobra made of metal on the front of his headdress as a symbol of his sovereignty."[1] The Hebrew word for "snake" is different in 7:9-10 from the one in 4:3. A related word (translated "monster") is used in Ezekiel 29:3 for Egypt and its pharaoh.

47

2. The magicians were able to imitate the trick of turning staffs into snakes (see 7:8-12). However, what do you think it signified that Aaron's staff swallowed theirs?

_____

_____

_____

_____

_____

3. In the left column of the following chart, list the first nine judgments (commonly called plagues) in 7:14–10:29.

Judgments	Losses

Judgments	Losses

4. In the chart above, put a star by each of the plagues that the Egyptian magicians could imitate.

5. In light of 8:19, what was the point of the magicians' involvement in these events?

_____

_____

For Thought and Discussion: Do you detect a sense of humor in the Lord's choice of plagues? Explain.

_____

_____

6. In the right column of the chart for question 3, write down what lasting (as opposed to temporary) losses the Egyptians incurred in each judgment.

7. "The Egyptians will know that I am the LORD when I stretch out my hand against Egypt and bring the Israelites out of it" (7:5). What do you think the Egyptians "knew" about "the LORD" after what 7:8–10:29 describes came to pass?

_____

_____

_____

Nile (7:17). Exodus 12:12 says the tenth plague is a "judgment on all the gods of Egypt." It completed what the first nine began, for they were also affronts to the Egyptian nature gods. The first plague judged Ha'pi, the Nile-god who supposedly saw to it that the river flooded at the right time, just enough to provide crucial water and renewed soil, and not so much that villages were inundated. The judgment on the Nile may have been an upset of the flood cycle to prove that Ha'pi was no real god.

Frogs (8:2). To ridicule the frog-goddess Heqit, who supposedly governed human fertility and assisted women in childbirth, the Lord deluged the land in filthy and then rotting frogs.

Livestock (9:3). "The Egyptians worshiped many animals and animal-headed deities, including the bull-gods Apis and Mnevis, the cow-god Hathor and the ram-god Khnum. Thus Egyptian religion is again rebuked and ridiculed."[2]

Darkness (10:21). An insult to the sun-god Ra (or Re), one of Egypt's chief deities.[3] (*Rameses* means "Ra is born.")

8. How does 6:28–10:29 illustrate Moses' submission to God and his unique authority over men?

_____

_____

_____

9. What lessons of leadership do you think Moses learned through his experience mediating between God and Pharaoh?

_____

_____

_____

_____

10. How did God show His care for Israel in the midst of the plagues (see 8:22-23, 9:4 7,26; 10:23)?

_____

_____

_____

_____

11. What was Israel supposed to learn from the plague-judgments, and how was she supposed to respond (see 5:21–6:8; 10:1-2)?

_____

_____

_____

_____

_____

_____

For Thought and Discussion: How are submission to God and authority over men related?

For Further Study: Study Jesus' teaching about authority and submission in the Gospels.

For Thought and Discussion: To what extent are Christians protected from the suffering in the world as Israel was protected when God judged Egypt? Why do you suppose this is so?

Optional Application: God revealed to Moses what He was going to do, but not a precise timetable or all the details. Are you acting with obedience like Moses to what God has told you? Are you patiently trusting and acting?

For Thought and Discussion:

a. Why couldn't Israel worship the Lord and stay in Egypt (see 5:1,3; 8:25-28)?

b. In the New Testament, Egypt symbolizes slavery to sin. Why can't Christians worship the Lord and stay in slavery to sin (see Romans 6:15-23)?

For Further Study:

a. Psalm 105:1-11,23-36 refers to the events of the exodus and how God's people should act in light of them.

b. Psalm 106:6-12 evaluates Israel's response to God's gracious intervention.

Your response

12. What insight from 6:28–10:29 seems most personally significant to you?

_____

_____

_____

_____

_____

13. How would you like this truth to affect your attitudes and habits?

_____

_____

_____

_____

_____

_____

14. What would you like to do about this truth this week?

_____

_____

_____

_____

15. List any questions you have about 6:28–10:29.

_____

_____

_____

_____

For the group

Warm-up. Ask several people to tell how God has demonstrated His power in their lives recently.

Read aloud and summarize. You probably won't want to read all of 6:28–10:29 aloud. Instead read just part of it, such as 7:1-7,14-24; 10:21-29. Then have someone summarize what happens in these chapters.

Questions. Don't spend time listing the plagues and the losses (questions 2 and 6). Instead, discuss the points God was making with the magicians, the staffs turned to the snakes, and all the plagues. What was God showing about Himself? What was He trying to get across to the Egyptian people and to His own people? How can you apply these lessons to yourselves?

Talk about the box "The Plagues" below if the group is interested, but don't allow an argument. The theory described there is largely speculation based on the idea that the Lord was ridiculing the root of Egyptian religion. Don't let anyone get the idea either that the theory is certain or that it questions the miraculous nature of the plagues.

Prayer. Praise the Lord who is supreme over all the forces of nature. Praise Him that there is no god but Him. Ask Him to write this truth on your hearts so that you will be utterly devoted to Him.

The Plagues

Some scholars think "[t]he first nine plagues may have been a series of miraculous intensifications of natural events taking place in less than a year, and coming at God's bidding and timing."[4] For example, the Nile normally flooded in late summer and early fall because of heavy rains at its source in Ethiopia. As Moses stretched out his staff, God may have sent an unseasonable flood. The "blood" in the river may have been huge quantities of red sediment or red algae washed down with the water (something similar happened in 2 Kings 3:22 at a prophet's cue). The bacteria-laden algae may

(continued on page 54)

(continued from page 53)

have killed the fish and made the water undrinkable. The frogs also could not survive, and at the Lord's word they swarmed out of the river. Gnats normally bred in the flooded fields, and they did so unseasonably and rapidly when the Lord commanded. As the Nile receded, flies found ideal breeding places in damp ground. The flies carried anthrax bacteria, which first infected the livestock, then gave skin anthrax (boils, abscesses) to the people. It was normal for a little rain or hail to occur after the flood season, but the Lord sent a terrible hailstorm hot on the heels of this strange acceleration of the yearly cycle. (The rain usually fell in the Delta region where Goshen was located and rarely in the rest of Egypt, but the Lord sent the storm everywhere but Goshen to make His control unmistakable.) Again, hot east winds usually followed the rain period and often brought locusts, so the Lord made an east wind bring a hoard of locusts next. The hot winds also often brought sandstorms from the desert, the ninth plague may have been a sandstorm so severe that it obscured the sun.[5]

This is a possible, though not certain, reconstruction of what happened. The rapid shift of seasons, each bringing its worst disaster and each timed to Moses' word, would certainly have frightened the Egyptians, whose religion was designed to appease nature gods and assure that the natural cycle stayed in balance. Clearly, the Lord, not the gods of Egypt, was really in control of nature.

1. Kenneth Barker, ed., *The NIV Study Bible* (Grand Rapids, MI: Zondervan, 1985), 91.
2. Barker, 98.
3. Kenneth Kitchen, "Plagues of Egypt," *The New Bible Dictionary*, 2nd ed., ed. J. D. Douglas, et. al. (Wheaton, IL: Tyndale, 1982), 944.
4. Barker, 96.
5. Barker, 96–100.

EXODUS 7:14–11:10

Judgments on Egypt: 2

Now that you've looked at the first nine judgments, take a closer look at some issues they raise.

Pharaoh's heart

1. Look back at your chart in question 3, and note the losses Egypt suffered after each of the first nine plagues. Below, write down Pharaoh's initial and final response to each judgment (see 7:22-23; 8:8,15,19,25-32; 9:7,12,27-28,34-35; 10:7-11,16-20,24-28). (You won't find any initial response in some cases.)

Pharaoh's initial response	Pharaoh's final response
Nile-blood	
frogs	

For Further Study: Research other passages that mention the plagues (Numbers 14:22; Deuteronomy 6:22; Joshua 9:9; 1 Samuel 4:8; Nehemiah 9:10; Psalm 43–51; Psalm 78:12; Jeremiah 32:20-21; Acts 7:36). What do these passages teach you about God and His purposes in the plagues?

<table>
<tr><td rowspan="2">**Optional Application:** Pharaoh relented under the pressure of the judgments, but when the immediate threat was over, he returned to his opposition to God. Do you make promises to God when in trouble that you disregard when things are okay?</td><td>Pharaoh's
initial response</td><td>Pharaoh's
final response</td></tr>
<tr><td>gnats</td><td></td></tr>
</table>

	Pharaoh's initial response	Pharaoh's final response
gnats		
flies		
livestock		
boils		
hail		
locusts		
darkness		

For Further Study: Observe the parallels between God's judgments on Egypt in Exodus and His judgments on the world in Revelation 8:1–9:21; 16:1-21. Why do you suppose Revelation echoes Exodus?

2. What indications are there that Pharaoh's conscience was affected by some of these plagues?

_____

_____

_____

_____

_____

Optional Application: How soft is your heart toward God's instructions? Pray for softening.

For Further Study: Read Romans 9:6-33 for the context of Paul's remarks about Pharaoh.

For Thought and Discussion: Does God's hardening of Pharaoh's heart imply that Pharaoh was not responsible for his opposition to God's plan? Does the Scripture's emphasis on God's sovereignty undercut human responsibility? Explain.

Study Skill — Hebrew Thought

Europeans and Americans are raised with a system of thought that originated in ancient Greece. This system stresses logic — the kind mathematicians use to deduce axioms in geometry, and the kind Sherlock Holmes made famous for solving crimes. Greek logic insists that opposites contradict each other and cannot both be true.

By contrast, Hebrews believed that opposites are often both true. In the Bible we find Jesus, the apostles, and the prophets often holding apparently conflicting ideas in tension. A prime example is divine sovereignty versus human responsibility. The box, "Pharaoh's Heart," examines how the Scriptures can say both that God hardened Pharaoh's heart and that Pharaoh hardened his own heart. This is a logical contradiction for Greek-minded people, but for the Hebrew mind it is a profound paradox to be held together. "Both . . . and," not "either/or," is often the biblical viewpoint.

---

3. In Hebrew thought, the heart is the core of a person—the seat of intellect, emotions, and will. What do you think it means to have a hard heart?

_____

_____

_____

_____

**For Thought and
Discussion:**
a. Why don't
miracles create faith?
(Compare Exodus
7:8–10:29 to Luke
16:19-31.)
b. What, then, are
the purposes of mira-
cles, such as those in
Exodus?

**For Thought
and Discussion:**
According to Romans
9:15-17, why is it
important to you
personally that God
is able to harden or
unharden hearts
that people have set
against Him?

For Further Study:
See the process of
hardening one's own
heart and then hav-

4. Why did God raise up a hardhearted pharaoh at this time (see 9:16)?

_____

_____

_____

_____

_____

5. What do you learn from the fact that under the first five plagues it is said that Pharaoh hardened his own heart, but under the sixth, eighth, and ninth it is said that the Lord hardened it?

_____

_____

_____

_____

_____

6. What compromises does Pharaoh eventually start offering (see 8:25-28; 10:8-11,24)?

_____

_____

_____

_____

_____

7. How does Moses respond in each case?

_____

_____

_____

_____

8. Do you think Moses' words in 10:9,26 are just a ploy to escape, or do they say something about the Lord's claims on Israel? Explain your view.

_____

_____

_____

_____

The tenth plague (11:1-10)

9. Describe the tenth and last plague (see 11:1-10).

_____

_____

_____

_____

10. What responsibility does each of the following have for bringing about the last plague (see 10:24–11:10)?

Pharaoh _____

_____

_____

_____

Moses _____

_____

_____

_____

God _____

_____

_____

_____

ing God harden it in Romans 1:18-32.

For Thought and Discussion: Are all, some, or no "natural" disasters divine judgments? Explain your reasoning. (Consider Matthew 24:6-8; Luke 13:1-5.)

Optional Application: Moses demanded Israel's freedom in order that God's people could serve Him, not so that they could indulge themselves. Do you ever use freedom as an opportunity to indulge your desires? Do you use your political and spiritual freedom as liberty to serve God, or to do as you please?

For Thought and Discussion:
a. Can you expect God to lead you in specific decisions as He informed Moses of the details of His plan as it unfolded? Why or why not?
b. What choices and actions did Moses take that made him able to receive God's instructions?

For Thought and Discussion: What should the Egyptian people have learned from the plague-judgments? How does this demonstrate God's mercy?

Your response

11. What truth reflected in 7:14–11:10 would you like to take to heart this week?

_____

_____

_____

_____

12. How would you like this to affect you?

_____

_____

_____

_____

_____

13. What steps can you take this week to act on this truth?

_____

_____

_____

14. List any questions you have about this lesson.

_____

_____

_____

For the group

Warm-up. Ask, "How do you feel about the idea of God having a decisive influence over the way people think and feel? Does this offend you, scare you, make you feel secure? Why?" Many people have strong feelings about

God's sovereignty; they are either strongly in favor of it or strongly opposed to it for reasons other than what biblical passages say. You may find it helpful to let everyone voice why he or she finds the idea encouraging or horrifying before you try to discuss the hardening of Pharaoh's heart. Some of the misconceptions you may find people holding deep down are:

1. God's sovereignty means I'm a helpless puppet.
2. God is too scary to have that much power; I need to feel in control of my life.
3. I don't want the responsibility of having any freedom to make choices; I am afraid to be wrong and be punished.
4. If I'm not responsible for my actions, I can do what I please and it's God's fault.

Questions. Letting people air their feelings may raise the temperature of the discussion. Try to diffuse hostility by focusing on what the text of Exodus *says*. How does each person account for the actual words that give responsibility to both Pharaoh and God? What signs of Pharaoh's freedom and moral responsibility do you see? What signs do you see of God's control over events?

As "Study Skill—Hebrew Thought" explains, you need not nail down a solution to this tension. Instead, explore the implications of human responsibility and divine sovereignty for your lives. Are you hardhearted in any areas? What responsibility does each of you have for responding to God today?

Prayer. Praise God for the mystery of His sovereignty that allows for human moral freedom and responsibility. Thank Him for not making you robots or puppets, and for not casting you adrift without His guidance. Ask Him to soften your hearts to hear, understand, love, and obey Him. As free people, give Him permission to act in your lives for your good and the good of others. Invite His control over your lives, trusting His wisdom.

Pharaoh's Heart

In spite of the variety and seriousness of the plagues, the witness of his own magicians as to their divine origin, and the distinction between

(continued on page 62)

(continued from page 61)

Egypt and Goshen, Pharaoh repeatedly hardened his heart (see 7:13-14,22; 8:15,19,32; 9:7,34-35) and refused to let Israel leave. Yet God not only predicted this would happen beforehand, but even promised He would cause it (see 4:21; 7:3), and the text says He did (see 9:12; 10:1,20,27; 11:10; 14:4,8). The apostle Paul said the hardening of Pharaoh's heart illustrated God's sovereign rule over everything (see Romans 9:15-18). The events of Exodus show God's control over not only physical forces but even men's hearts.

This has caused much controversy throughout Church history. Some argue that God foresaw that Pharaoh would harden his heart and thus only confirmed what was in reality Pharaoh's free choice. To believe that God would harden a person makes God unjust, they claim, and even threatens the preaching of the gospel. If God has already determined what every person's response to Him will be, what is the point of witnessing for Christ?

"The precise relationship between [divine] sovereignty and [human] freedom cannot be dogmatically stated."[1] Yet faith in God's sovereignty is our only real ground for hope. Because people are "dead" in their sins, and their wills are subject to corrupt and deluded hearts, God must intervene if anyone is to respond to Him (see Romans 9:15; Ephesians 2:1-5; 4:17-19). We rejoice that the scope of God's love is not narrow, but as broad as the world for which Christ died.

1. Bernard Ramm, *Protestant Biblical Interpretation* (Grand Rapids, MI: Baker, 1970), 171.

EXODUS 12:1-51

Last Night in Egypt

For some four centuries, Abraham's descendants have labored in a foreign land. Now, in a single night they will exchange bondage for freedom, rags for the riches of Egypt, the prison of Goshen for the road to the Promised Land. Read 12:1-51.

1. Chapter 12 describes Israel's departure from Egypt and the feast that commemorates it. Which of these receives more space, and why do you suppose it does?

   _____

   _____

   _____

   _____

2. The Passover feast was to be prepared according to divinely revealed instructions. Summarize the directions God gave regarding . . .

   the time (see 12:2-3,6) _____

   _____

   _____

   _____

   the menu—its main dish (see 12:3-5) _____

   _____

For Thought and Discussion:
   a. Upon what conditions could a foreigner associate himself with God's people (see 12:48-49)?
   b. Why was this necessary?
   c. From 12:37-38, 48-49, in what ways was Israel a closed community and in what ways was it open?

For Further Study:
The Passover is con-
nected with some key
events in Israel's later
history (see Numbers
9:1-14; Joshua 5:10-12;
2 Kings 23:21-23; 2
Chronicles 30:1–31:1;
Ezra 6:19-22; Matthew
26:17-29).

the menu—its manner of preparation (see 12:8-10)

_____

_____

the menu—its side dishes (see 12:8) _____

_____

the menu—ingredients excluded (see 12:14-20)

_____

_____

preparations for the home where the feast is
held (see 12:7,22) _____

_____

_____

_____

_____

the attire required (see 12:11) _____

_____

_____

the purpose of the ceremony (see 12:12-13,23)

_____

_____

_____

_____

the participants required and excluded
(see 12:43-49) _____

_____

_____

_____

_____

Study Skill — Types

A *type* is an Old Testament person, object, or event that God designed to resemble its anti-type in the New Testament. God gave types to prepare Israel to understand Christ and to be moral and doctrinal examples for us (see 1 Corinthians 10:6,11; Hebrews 10:1). In some cases the New Testament explicitly states that something in the Old Testament is a type (see Hebrews 7:3; 9:8-9; 11:19; 1 Peter 3:21). At other times it does not. Some interpreters fall into error by abusing typology, but we can avoid foolish mistakes if we keep some principles in mind.

1. "No doctrine or theory should ever be built upon a type or types independently of direct teaching elsewhere in Scripture." Types are meant to illustrate, amplify, and illuminate doctrines taught explicitly elsewhere.

2. "The parallelism between type and antitype should not be pressed to fanciful extremes." Not every detail in a story (such as the exodus), nor every detail about a person (such as Moses), is parallel to its antitype.[1]

The whole narrative of Israel's exodus from Egypt is a type of how Jesus liberates people from slavery to sin. Most importantly, the Passover lamb is a type of Christ. Paul tells us this explicitly (see 1 Corinthians 5:7). Therefore, it is worthwhile to look at what Exodus says about the Passover to see how it illuminates Christ's work.

Optional Application: Meditate daily this week on the implications of the fact that Christ is your Passover Lamb. How can you act in light of this fact? How can you express your gratitude in concrete ways?

3. Since Christ is the ultimate fulfillment of the Passover, what does it tell us about His work that . . .

the lamb had to be "without defect" (see Exodus 12:5; compare 1 Peter 1:19)?

_____

_____

_____

_____

65

**Optional
Application:** The
Israelites had to do
certain things to
appropriate God's
promise to redeem
them — put lamb's
blood on their door-
frames, eat a meal,
and actually walk out
of Egypt. What do
you need to do this
week to act in faith
and appropriate what
God has promised
you?

**Optional
Application:** What
difference should it
make to your actions
this week that God
has redeemed you
from slavery?

the blood of the lamb, smeared on the doorframes
of a family's house, protected the occupants from
God's deadly wrath (see Exodus 12:7,13; compare
1 Thessalonians 1:10; Hebrews 9:22)?

_____

_____

_____

_____

the Passover was also a feast of fellowship with,
thanks to, and nourishment from God for
the journey to Canaan; and the lamb was the
main course of the feast (see Exodus 12:8-11;
compare John 6:51-58)?

_____

_____

_____

_____

_____

First month (12:2). Most ancient cultures had agricultural calendars and began their years in the
season of new life in nature. Israel's agricultural
calendar began in the fall, the beginning of the
rainy season (not spring, as in North America).
But now God says that the nation's religious
calendar will begin in the spring because its
religion will be based not on agriculture but on
this historic act of redemption from slavery.

Roast (12:9). Wandering shepherds roasted meat;
only settled farmers would cook it in water, and
raw meat was a feature of pagan rites.

Festival of Unleavened Bread (12:17). This was
partly distinct from, but connected with, the
Passover. It began with the Passover meal and
continued for seven more days.

66

4. What did getting rid of yeast during the seven-day feast after Passover represent (see 12:33-34,39)?

_____

_____

_____

_____

_____

5. What does getting rid of the yeast in order to celebrate the Passover symbolize for Christians (see Luke 12:1; 1 Corinthians 5:8)?

_____

_____

_____

_____

_____

6. Even more than the first nine plagues, at whom was the last judgment directed (see 12:12)?

_____

_____

_____

7. Why do you think the Israelites had to do something to protect themselves from God's judgment? Why didn't the Lord automatically exempt the whole territory in which His people were living, as He had done in the previous plagues?

_____

_____

_____

_____

_____

For Thought and Discussion: Why did God forbid Israel to break the bones of the Passover lamb (see Exodus 12:46; John 19:36)?

Optional Application: Is there yeast in your life? How can you work on getting rid of it this week?

For Thought and Discussion: Is there any indication in Exodus 1–12 that Israel was morally superior to Egypt? What does this suggest about God's grace?

**For Thought
and Discussion:**
"Liberation Theology"
interprets Exodus as
teaching that God is
concerned for and
on the side of all the
oppressed peoples in
the world. How would
you evaluate this
interpretation?

8. Why did God make the final judgment, like the rest, universal to all classes in Egypt (see 11:4-5; 12:29-30)?

_____

_____

_____

9. Why did God make such a big deal about the Israelites asking the Egyptians for silver, gold, and clothing (see 3:21-22; 11:2-3; 12:35-36)?

_____

_____

_____

10. In your judgment, was this theft or extortion, or was it justified? Why?

_____

_____

_____

_____

11. What does 12:1-51 show you about God's character and priorities?

_____

_____

_____

Your response

12. What aspect of 12:1-51 would you like to concentrate on this week?

_____

_____

_____

_____

13. What difference would you like this to make to
your life?

_____

_____

_____

14. How can you act on this truth this week?

_____

_____

_____

15. List any questions you have about 12:1-51.

_____

_____

_____

For the group

Warm-up. Over the next several weeks, give each
group member a chance to share how God brought
him or her out of slavery into freedom in Christ.
Depending on how much time it takes, you could
hear one or two people's stories each week as a
warm-up to your meeting. Ask the people to be
brief. Some members may feel that they have no
story to tell because they were raised Christian, but
they may not be aware that God drew them, too,
however gradual it felt.

Questions. Don't labor tediously through all the
observations in question 2, unless the group had
trouble with this. Instead, use your time to explore
what the Passover and exodus reveal about God's

eternal character and how they illuminate what Christ has done for you.

Prayer. Thank God for bringing each of you out of slavery and for protecting you from His judgment by the blood of Christ. Pray special thanks for the person who shared his or her story of redemption. Ask the Lord to impress on each of you how to live in light of your deliverance this week.

Passover and Exodus

The rest of the Old Testament affirms that the first Passover and the departure from Egypt were Israel's real birthday as a nation. References to these events run throughout the Hebrew Scriptures (see Leviticus 19:36; Numbers 20:16; Deuteronomy 1:27; Joshua 24:6; Judges 2:1; 1 Samuel 8:8; 2 Samuel 7:6; 1 Kings 8:16; 2 Kings 17:36; 1 Chronicles 17:21; 2 Chronicles 6:5; Nehemiah 9:18; Psalm 81:10; Jeremiah 2:6; Ezekiel 20:10; Daniel 9:15; Hosea 11:1; Amos 2:10; Micah 6:4; Haggai 2:5).

Before the Passover and exodus, the descendants of Abraham, Isaac, and Jacob were a people, yet they hardly knew what that meant. Only as God worked through Moses did the Israelites begin to comprehend something of who they really were. In their miraculous liberation, they were brought face to face with the grace of God as the foundation of their life.

For this reason, the Passover and exodus are to Old Testament Israel what the cross of Christ is to the New Testament church. Both events created a radically new situation. Yet just as only those who respond in faith to Christ's death can truly enjoy its benefits, so only those Israelites who had true faith in the Lord were really His people. The Bible's message is consistent: God's power can revolutionize our circumstances, but only as we trust Him fully do we become His children.

1. J. Sidlow Baxter, *Explore the Book*, vol. 1 (Grand Rapids, MI: Zondervan, 1966), 55–56.

EXODUS 13:1–15:21
Consecration, Salvation, Celebration

Now the Lord brings to a glorious conclusion the deliverance of His people. This portion of the story climaxes God's judgments on Egypt and gives us a first glimpse of Israel's response to God's leadership through Moses. As you read 13:1–15:21, be aware of the mood in each section of the drama.

Consecration (13:1-16)

1. God commanded Moses to consecrate to Him all the firstborn persons and domesticated animals of Israel. What did this involve (see 13:1-2,11-16)?

_____

_____

_____

_____

2. By what right did the Lord demand this of His people (see 13:14-16)?

_____

_____

_____

_____

For Thought and Discussion: The Lord gave Israel certain traditions by which to commemorate the exodus each year. What traditions has He given the body of Christ to commemorate His saving work?

71

For Thought and Discussion:
a. The command to consecrate the firstborn took effect only when Israel entered the Promised Land (see 13:11-16). Why does God fulfill His promises before He even asks us to do things for Him?
b. What specific things has the Lord done for you that make you want to please Him?

Consecrate (13:2). The Hebrew term is sometimes translated "sanctify." It indicates an action whereby someone or something is dedicated to God and so considered holy.[1]

Hand . . . forehead (13:9). God intended this as a figure of speech to show how vividly the Feast of Unleavened Bread should remind Israel of God's grace and Law. However, later Jews have taken this and similar verses literally. They write Exodus 13:1-10; 13:11-16; Deuteronomy 6:49; 11:13-21 on separate strips of paper and put them in two small leather boxes. A man binds these boxes (called "phylacteries" in Matthew 23:5 or *tephillim* in Hebrew) on his forehead and left arm before beginning his morning prayers.

Law (13:9). We often think of the Law as primarily the Ten Commandments and the other detailed regulations in the Pentateuch. However, "law" (Hebrew: *torah*) does not mean only rules and regulations. It means "teaching," and it encompasses all that God has revealed about Himself and done for His people. The Jews call all of the Pentateuch (Genesis through Deuteronomy) the *Torah*. In the New Testament, we even find the whole Hebrew Bible called the Law.

The command to have the Law *on your lips* comes in the context of an instruction to tell one's children how God liberated Israel from Egypt (see 13:8,14-15). So, to have the Law on one's lips means not primarily talking about the Lord's commands, but what He has revealed about Himself and done for His people.

Redeem (13:13). Recall the definition from 6:6. The redemption price of each person in Israel was set later (see Numbers 3:44-48). God told Moses to count each member of the eleven tribes, then to count each member of the tribe of Levi. God claimed the Levites for His special service, and each member of that tribe counted as the redemption price for one firstborn male of the other tribes. Each firstborn male Israelite left over had to pay five shekels of silver to ransom his life.

3. By redeeming (buying) Israel from slavery and sparing its firstborn from judgment, the Lord became each person's new owner. He reminded the Israelites of His claim by making them consecrate the life of each firstborn male to Him. How do the following New Testament passages portray the Christian's situation in a similar light?

Romans 6:17-18,22 _____

_____

_____

Romans 12:1 _____

_____

1 Corinthians 6:20 _____

_____

4. Do you think the fact that the Lord claimed all the firstborn animals meant that the Israelites could regard the rest of their possessions as their own? Why or why not?

_____

_____

_____

_____

Optional Application: What aspects of your life should you take special care to consecrate to the Lord this week?

Crossing the sea (13:17–14:31)

5. What factors did God take into account in selecting Israel's route to Canaan (see 13:17)?

_____

_____

_____

_____

For Thought and Discussion:
a. How does the text describe the Israelites' condition as they came from Egypt (see 13:18)?
b. Do the Israelites use their arms in chapter 14? What's the point, then, of mentioning them?

Philistine (13:17). Three times (see 3:8,17; 13:5), the Lord has listed the inhabitants of Canaan whom Israel will dispossess. Now He adds another group, the Philistines. The Canaanites, Hittites, and so on are named elsewhere as the groups Israel must destroy along with their religions because of their debauched, idolatrous practices (see Exodus 34:13; Numbers 33:52,55; Deuteronomy 7:1). The Philistines, on the other hand, are never included in these lists, nor is their religion singled out for condemnation like those of the other groups. Apparently, the Philistines did not represent the same spiritual danger to Israel that the Canaanites did for two reasons: (1) their religion, though idolatrous, did not include the same licentious practices; and (2) they never intermarried indiscriminately with the Israelites as the Canaanites did.

The origins of the Philistines and Canaanites also differed. While the Canaanites were indigenous to Palestine, the Philistines came from somewhere in or around the Mediterranean sometime between 1300 and 1200 BC.[2]

If they face war (13:17). The direct route from Goshen to Canaan "was heavily guarded by a string of Egyptian fortresses."[3]

6. What was the sign of God's presence with His people, and what did it do for them (see 13:20-22)?

_____

_____

_____

_____

7. Why did the Lord position Israel by the sea (see 14:2-4)?

_____

_____

_____

74

8. Since God had already liberated Israel, why do you think He was still concerned with Pharaoh and the Egyptians?

_____

_____

_____

_____

_____

9. How did the Israelites react to the Egyptian threat (see 14:10-12)? Explain in your own words.

_____

_____

_____

_____

_____

10. How did Moses respond (see 14:13-14)?

_____

_____

_____

_____

_____

_____

11. Describe how God saved His people (see 14:15-28).

_____

_____

_____

_____

_____

_____

For Thought and Discussion: Should modern human oppressors expect the same treatment from God as Pharaoh received, or was this a unique situation? Explain your reasoning.

Optional Application:
a. Compare 14:10-12 to 2:14 and 5:21. Do you ever react to crises like this?

b. Is the outcome of Israel's crisis an encouragement to you? Can you apply 14:15?

For Thought and Discussion: Pharaoh and his army are types of Satan and his army, who want to re-enslave Christians to sin. What can you conclude from Exodus 14:1–15:21 about God's plans in your world and your life for Satan and sin? How should you act in light of this?

For Thought and Discussion: Why do you think God instructed Moses to perform visible symbolic gestures to unleash His miraculous power (see 14:16,26)?

For Thought and Discussion: How is the progressive nature of God's revelation and intervention apparent in chapter 14?

Red Sea (13:18). Identifying its precise location has proven difficult. Scholars are divided on Israel's precise route from Egypt to Canaan. While archaeology has been able to pinpoint some places mentioned in Exodus, others are still uncertain.

The term "Red Sea" was a general one used to designate the whole body of water to the east of Egypt and the Sudan. (Ancient Greek writers even called the Indian Ocean "the Red Sea"![4]) The Hebrew text of Exodus uses the term *Yam Suph*, which means "Sea of [papyrus] Reeds." The Greek translation of the Old Testament made in 200 BC renders this as "Red Sea." This sea, which Israel crossed in fleeing Pharaoh's army, has been identified with at least four different sites: Lake Menzaleh or Lake Sibonis, both on Egypt's northern border (see the map); the Bitter Lakes region, or the Gulf of Suez. Which of these locations best fits with the biblical and archaeological evidence? There is no majority opinion. The Gulf of Suez is salt water, so papyrus reeds do not grow there. But any of the bodies of water north to the Mediterranean could have been called "Sea of Reeds." Since Egypt's geography may have changed in 3500 years, we can't precisely pinpoint the spot where a reedy lake was large and deep enough to drown a whole army.[5]

Celebration (15:1-21)

12. The text notes how Israel's faith grew through this experience (see 14:31), then describes how the nation praised God (see 15:1-21). What point do you think the Holy Spirit is making here?

_____

_____

_____

_____

_____

13. Israel's song of praise can be divided into two main parts: 15:1-12 and 15:14-18, with verse 13

serving as a transition between them. How is God pictured in each part of the song?

15:1-12 _____

_____

_____

_____

_____

_____

_____

15:14-18 _____

_____

_____

_____

_____

14. How would you summarize the message of . . .

15:1-12? _____

_____

_____

15:14-18? _____

_____

_____

the whole song? _____

_____

_____

_____

_____

_____

Optional Application: Choose a piece of the song in 15:1-21 to memorize, meditate on, and act on. For instance, what does it imply for your life that God is your strength and your song (see verse 2)? That He is a warrior (see verse 3)? That there is no one like Him in holiness and glory (see verse 11)? That He will reign forever (see verse 18)?

For Further Study:
How does Exodus
12:1–15:21 partly fulfill
Genesis 12:1-3?

Your response

15. How would you summarize the theme of
    13:1–15:21?

    _____

    _____

    _____

    _____

Study Skill — Application
Instead of reading a passage of Scripture for
what God is really saying in it, people sometimes try to find in it a message for their current
situation. However, not every instruction in a
narrative passage is immediately relevant to
you. For example, in 14:15, Moses tells Israel to
be still and watch what God is going to do. But
in other passages, Moses tells Israel to fight (see
17:8-13). Without listening to the Holy Spirit and
taking counsel with other Christians, you have
no way of knowing which of these (if either) is
God's command to you in your current circumstances. Instead of using specific commands
directed at Israel as oracles for you, try to build
your applications on the eternal message of the
passage. If you feel that a specific command
is a personal word to you, proceed cautiously.
Ask the Lord to send objective evidence (other
believers, other passages of Scripture, facts in
the situation that match facts in the narrative) to
confirm that this is His instruction for you now.

---

16. What one insight from 13:1–15:21 would you
    like to take to heart this week?

    _____

    _____

    _____

17. How would you like this truth to affect the way you live?

_____

_____

_____

_____

18. What can you do about this?

_____

_____

_____

_____

19. List any questions you have about 13:1–15:21.

_____

_____

_____

_____

For the group

Warm-up. Ask one or two more people to tell the stories of their deliverance briefly. If this seems to be time-consuming, let each person describe just one episode in the process of his or her deliverance.

Questions. This lesson covers three chapters at breakneck speed. Feel free to take two meetings to discuss it or to cover some sections lightly. Don't be diverted into a debate about the location of the Red Sea; the miracle is a fact, whatever the site.

Prayer. Use 15:1-21 as a springboard to praise and worship. You may even know some songs based on these verses. Ask the Lord to impress His majesty, holiness, and glory upon you so that you will trust Him as your deliverer.

1. T. E. McComiskey, "be hallowed, holy, sanctified . . ." *Theological Wordbook of the Old Testament*, vol. 2, ed. R. L. Harris, et al. (Chicago: Moody, 1980), 786–787.
2. W. S. LaSor, D. A. Hubbard, and F. W. Bush, *Old Testament Survey* (Grand Rapids, MI: Eerdmans, 1982), 121–122.
3. Kenneth Barker, ed., *The NIV Study Bible* (Grand Rapids, MI: Zondervan, 1985), 105.
4. "Redemption," *The Eerdmans Bible Dictionary,* ed. Allen C. Meyers, et. al. (Grand Rapids, MI: Eerdmans, 1987), 876.
5. J. J. Davis, *Moses and the Gods of Egypt* (Grand Rapids, MI: Baker, 1971), 171; Barry J. Beitzel, *The Moody Atlas of Bible Lands* (Chicago: Moody, 1985), 90; T. V. Briscoe, "Route of the Exodus," *The International Standard Bible Encyclopedia*, vol. 2, ed. Geoffrey W. Bromiley (Grand Rapids, MI: Eerdmans, 1982), 240–241.

EXODUS 15:22–17:7
Grumbling and Grace

The Israelites were free from Egypt and Pharaoh's pursuing host. But as drama gave way to the drudgery of a wasteland journey, the people's song of praise changed to a string of complaints. The Israelites had seen the results of Pharaoh's hard heart; would they do better?

Read 15:22–17:7. On the map, trace Israel's journey in this passage.

Fifteenth day of the second month (16:1). Exactly one month had passed since Israel's departure from Egypt.

---

1. Israel grumbles three times in 15:22–17:7. About what do the people complain in . . .

   15:23-24? _____

   _____

   16:2-3? _____

   _____

   17:1-3? _____

   _____

For Thought and Discussion:
   a. How could the Israelites, who believed in God and Moses after the Red Sea miracle, (see 14:31) show such faithlessness only a few days later (see 15:22-24)?
   b. What does this say about faith based primarily on miraculous signs?

81

For Thought and Discussion: Read how Psalm 95 and Hebrews 3 view the events at Massah. What is involved in a person hardening his or her heart, and what are the spiritual consequences of this?

Optional Application: Are you focused on the past like Israel, or the future like the Lord? Are you grumbling or trustfully praying and taking action in your current situation? How can you take Israel's example to heart?

2. What attitudes really lay behind these complaints (see 16:8; 17:7)?

_____

_____

_____

_____

3. Yet, they directed their grumbling at Moses and Aaron (see 15:24; 16:2; 17:2). Why do you think they did this?

_____

_____

_____

_____

_____

4. In voicing their complaints, with what did they compare their situation (see 16:3; 17:3)?

_____

_____

_____

_____

5. In your judgment, how valid was this comparison, and why?

_____

_____

_____

_____

6. The people were focused on present discomfort and past security. How does this compare to the Lord's perspective (see 3:7-8,13-17; 6:2-8; 13:3-10)?

_____

_____

_____

_____

_____

7. Put yourself in Israel's place, traveling for three days without water and ending up in yet another place with bad water (see 15:22-23). Imagine yourself hiking every day for a month on scant food rations with no meat (see 16:1-3). What attitudes and words do you think you would have for your human leaders and God?

_____

_____

_____

_____

_____

For Thought and Discussion: What was the Lord saying by bringing Israel to Elim right after the water crisis at Marah (see 15:27)?

For Thought and Discussion: What about the manna proved it was from God and for Israel?

A ruling and instruction (15:25). Technical terms that probably refer to 15:26.
_____

8. These experiences with water and food were tests for Israel. What was God testing (see 15:25-26; 16:4)?

_____

_____

_____

9. If Israel passed this test, what did God promise (see 15:26)?

_____

_____

_____

For Further Study:
How does Paul
apply Exodus 16:28
to Christians (see
2 Corinthians 8:15)?

**For Thought and
Discussion:**
a. God provided
rest without let-
ting His people go
hungry to get it (see
16:5,22-30). What was
this meant to teach
Israel about labor and
leisure?

b. Is there a
proper balance of
these in your life?
Reflect on this.

**Optional
Application:** Are you
setting the rest of
the body of Christ an
example of faith, or
are you going along
with the grumbling?
Think of one thing
you can do to help
another Christian
escape the pattern of
complaining.

10. What was unusual about the collection of the manna?

16:17-18 _____

_____

_____

_____

16:19-26 _____

_____

_____

_____

_____

11. What lessons do you think God intended Israel to learn from each of these?

_____

_____

_____

_____

_____

_____

_____

12. How did the case of the manna test Israel as you wrote in question 8 (see 16:4-30)?

_____

_____

_____

_____

_____

_____

84

13. How well did Israel pass the test?

_____

_____

_____

_____

14. The situation at Massah-Meribah was also about testing or proving. How was this testing (see 17:2,7) different from the testings at Marah (see 15:25-26) and the Desert of Sin (see 16:4)?

_____

_____

_____

_____

_____

For Thought and Discussion: Why is it okay for God to test us, but not okay for us to test Him?

For Thought and Discussion: What are the similarities and differences between the provision of bread and the two provisions of water?

For Thought and Discussion: Why do you think God led Israel in the manner 15:22–17:7 describes? What was He trying to achieve?

Study Skill — The Structure of the Narrative
It is important not only to look at an incident on its own, but also to notice how it relates to the events recorded before and after it. The author of Exodus, for instance, does not tell us everything that happened (compare John 21:25). Under the Spirit's guidance, he selects and groups events to make a point.

For example, all three episodes in 15:22–17:7 deal with Israel's complaints about physical necessities. The first and third are brief scenes about water, the middle one is a long incident about bread. If we miss the careful arrangement of these episodes, we might think they are just repetitive. We need to observe both the similarities and the differences, the comparisons and the contrasts, to grasp what the Holy Spirit is saying.

One theme that runs through all three scenes is testing. Yet the test is a little different in each case. What does this tell us? To answer this, we relate this passage to what we know about the whole book. Exodus is about how

(continued on page 86)

For Thought and Discussion: a. How does Exodus 7–17 portray God's sovereignty over physical creation, especially water?

b. Why do you think God stresses this power to Israel?

For Thought and Discussion: a. Does God provide physical bread and water for you today? What about spiritual bread and water (see John 4:13-14; 6:53-58)?

b. Are you trusting God for your physical and spiritual nourishment? How are you actively showing this trust?

c. Does trusting God mean we don't have to do anything to appropriate what He provides? Why or why not?

For Thought and Discussion: What do you think Moses learned from his experiences in 15:22–17:7?

(continued from page 85)

God transformed Israel from men's slaves to God's servants. In 1:1–15:21, that transformation involved primarily miracles to judge Egypt and liberate Israel. Those miracles scared Pharaoh, but just as importantly, they taught Israel that God could be trusted. In 15:22, a new stage of the transformation process began. Although physically free, the Israelites still had a slave mentality. And they still didn't trust their new master. The three episodes in 15:22–17:7 quickly paint for us the problem God was dealing with at this stage (renovating Israel inwardly from slaves to sons and daughters), and how He was going about it.

When you study Old or New Testament narratives, examine each scene on its own carefully. But don't forget to look at it alongside the scenes before and after it, and in the context of the whole book.

15. How did Moses react each time the people complained and argued with him (see 15:25; 16:6-7; 17:2-3)?

_____

_____

_____

16. Exodus 17:1-4 shows a total breakdown of trust between Israel and Moses—the people were ready to stone him. How did God go about restoring the nation's respect for Moses' authority (see 17:5-6)?

_____

_____

_____

_____

17. What should Israel have learned about the Lord from the experiences in 15:22–17:7? (Consider

86

Exodus 15:25-27; 16:7-12; 17:7; Deuteronomy 8:2-3.)

_____

_____

_____

_____

_____

_____

Your response

18. What truth from 15:22–17:7 seems most personally relevant to you right now?

_____

_____

_____

_____

_____

19. What would you like to do about it?

_____

_____

_____

_____

_____

_____

20. List any questions you have about 15:22–17:7.

_____

_____

_____

For Further Study:
Exodus 15:22–17:7 is important enough to be mentioned repeatedly later in the Bible. Study the lessons later authors drew (see Deuteronomy 6:16; 8:2-5; Nehemiah 9:19-21; Psalm 78:12-31; 81:1-16; 95:7-11; 105:37-42; 106:13-15; 136:16; Jeremiah 2:6; Ezekiel 20:10-20; Hosea 13:5-6; Amos 2.10; 5:25; John 6:25-59; Acts 7:36; 13:17-18; 1 Corinthians 10:5; Hebrews 3:7-19).

For Further Study:
Read other passages that describe Israel's unbelief during her wanderings (see Numbers 11:1-35; 13:16–14:45; 16:1-50; 20:2-13; 21:4-9; 25:1-18).

87

For Thought and Discussion: Does 15:22–17:7 portray leadership as a privilege or a burden? Explain.

_____

_____

For the group

Warm-up. Continue to share your experiences of deliverance.

Questions. You could spend your whole discussion on testing, or on what the incident with the manna taught Israel, or on some other issue this passage raises. Be sure to save time to discuss how you want to take these scenes to heart and act on them.

Prayer. Thank God for providing your physical and spiritual nourishment. Ask Him to help you trust Him enough to obey Him totally, even when He gives seemingly inexplicable instructions (see 16:19-20,25-29), and even when He seems to be slow in providing what you think you need. Pray for any group members facing serious struggles with trusting God (perhaps someone is out of work or ill or just has trouble relying on God).

EXODUS 17:8–18:27

War and Peace

Born and bred in Egypt, the Israelites were unpre-
pared for the rigors of desert travel. The first weeks
of scarce food and water strained their faith almost
to the breaking point. Only God's gracious intervention prevented riot and killing thirst, just as
it had saved Israel from Pharaoh's troops. But the
wilderness harbored other dangers as deadly as
drought and famine. And Moses found that the
demands of peace could be every bit as wearying as
those of war.

War with Amalek (17:8-16)

Amalekites (17:8). A group of Bedouin tribes who
lived in the desert south of Canaan. Since they
occupied the southern approach to Canaan and
had presumably heard that Israel was marching that way, they sent a detachment of soldiers
down to Rephidim to forestall the Israelites
before they could make trouble.[1]

Joshua (17:9). His name means "the LORD saves."
The Greek form of his name is *Iesous*, from
which we get the English "Jesus." Joshua was
Moses' aide, and a fine general.

1. By what two means did Israel defeat Amalek?

For Further Study:
Learn more about Joshua's preparation for leadership in Exodus 24:13; 32:17; 33:11; Numbers 11:26-30; 13:8-16; 14:5-9; 27:12-21; 32:28-30; 34:16-17; Deuteronomy 1:37-38; 3:21-29; 31:3-8,14-23.

_____

_____

_____

_____

2. What do you think was the point of Moses raising his staff and his hands?

_____

_____

_____

_____

_____

3. What does 17:8-13 imply about Moses?

_____

_____

_____

_____

4. What was Moses told to write down for Joshua's benefit (see 17:14)?

_____

_____

_____

_____

5. Why do you think this was so important to record?

_____

_____

For Thought and
Discussion: Because
of Amalek's unpro-
voked attack on
Israel, it became a
permanent object
of God's wrath. How
do the actions and
character of one
generation affect the
spiritual condition
and destiny of its
descendants? Is the
case of Amalek typi-
cal or atypical?

6. Consider what God promised to do to Amalek
(see 17:14,16). What does this suggest about the
relationship between the Lord and Israel?

_____

_____

_____

_____

_____

_____

7. In response to the battle with Amalek, Moses
built an altar (see 17:15). In your own words,
explain the meaning of the altar's name.

_____

_____

_____

_____

_____

Treaty with Jethro (18:1-27)

Brought (18:12). "The verb means 'provided' an
animal for sacrifice . . . not 'officiated at' a
sacrifice."[2]

Eat a meal with (18:12). A gesture of friendship. A
meal often sealed a treaty (covenant). Salt was a
symbol of fidelity (the compound doesn't break
down), so to "eat salt" with someone was to swear
loyalty to him. Bread always contained salt, so eat-
ing bread together implied the same thing.

For Thought and Discussion:
    a. How is Moses a good example for Christian leaders in 17:10-12; 18:13-26?
    b. What does he do that leaders should avoid?

8. What contrasts and similarities do you see between 18:1-27 and 17:8-16?

   contrasts_____

   _____

   _____

   _____

   _____

   _____

   _____

   similarities _____

   _____

   _____

   _____

   _____

   _____

9. Why could Israel make a covenant of friendship with Jethro (see 18:9-12)?

   _____

   _____

   _____

   _____

   _____

10. What aspects of Moses' personality does 18:13-16 reveal?

   _____

   _____

   _____

   _____

   _____

92

11. What does 18:24 show about Moses?

_____

_____

_____

_____

_____

12. Summarize Jethro's advice (see 18:17-23).

_____

_____

_____

_____

_____

13. Why was this good counsel? What benefits did it provide for Moses and Israel?

_____

_____

_____

_____

_____

14. How is this situation relevant for Christians?

_____

_____

_____

_____

_____

_____

For Thought and Discussion:
a. What qualities for a leader does Exodus 18:21 state?
b. Compare the qualities in Acts 6:3.

Optional Application:
a. How could your church or community apply what 17:10-12 and 18:13-26 illustrate about leadership?
b. Do you meet the standards for a leader in 18:21? How can you grow in this area?

For Thought and Discussion:
a. What can you learn about teamwork from 17:8–18:27?
b. Is it generally true that sharing responsibility ultimately weakens or strengthens authority? Why do you think so?

For Thought and Discussion: How did appointing others to help Moses help Israel to mature spiritually? Is this a widely applicable principle? Why or why not?

Optional Application: Although God was using Moses powerfully, he still listened to Jethro and took his advice. With what attitude do you hear correction and criticism?

Optional Application: Sacrifice was part of both war and peace for Israel (see 17:15; 18:12). Is worship part of your daily life, or something isolated? Find time today for praise and thanksgiving, and plan ways of building worship into your life.

Your response

15. What aspect of 17:8–18:27 would you like to take to heart?

_____

_____

_____

_____

_____

16. How would you like this to affect your attitudes and habits?

_____

_____

_____

_____

_____

17. What steps can you take to act on this desire?

_____

_____

_____

_____

_____

18. List any questions you have about 17:8–18:27.

_____

_____

_____

_____

For the group

Warm-up. If you haven't finished sharing your experiences of deliverance, keep on with that. If you have, ask, "Do you tend to operate on your own, or do you generally do things with a team?" Go around the room, letting each person respond. Individualism is rampant today; your group should be a place where people learn to trust and accomplish things with others. As leader, set an example by delegating responsibilities to group members (see 18:17-18). Encourage members to support each other in your efforts to apply Exodus by praying for and listening to one another. Look for ways to help each other actively, or think of how you can support your pastor or other leader.

Questions. Umberto Cassuto (page 212) mentions eight similarities between 17:8-16 and 18:1-27 — (1) the idea of coming to Israel for either war or peace; (2) the choice of men for certain tasks; (3) Moses sitting in a position of authority; (4) literal or spiritual "heaviness" (see 17:12; 18:18); (5) standing (see 17:9; 18:14); (6) the entire day until evening (see 17:12; 18:14); (7) the following day (see 17:9; 18:13); and (8) future events (see 17:16; 18:23). Which of these are significant?

Prayer. Pray for your leaders. Ask the Lord to help each of you unlearn individualism, learn to accept help and criticism, and make a habit of giving help whenever you see a need.

1. Umberto Cassuto, *A Commentary of the Book of Exodus* (Jerusalem: The Magnes Press, 1967), 204.
2. Kenneth Barker, ed., *The NIV Study Bible* (Grand Rapids, MI: Zondervan, 1985), 113.

EXODUS 19:1–20:21
Laws for a Priestly People

When the Israelites found themselves thrust out of Egypt into the desert waste, their freedom seemed to spell nothing but deprivation. The wilderness lacked even those few necessities they had taken for granted in the land of slavery. God graciously supplied their physical needs, but He was more concerned with the emptiness in their hearts than with the cravings of their stomachs. At Sinai He granted Israel an identity that would provide substance to the liberty He had bestowed. Read 19:1–20:21.

For Thought and Discussion: Why do you think God chose such an isolated place for His revelation?

For Thought and Discussion: What does the illustration of eagles' wings (see 19:4) suggest about God's actions?

Consecration (19:1-25)

Sinai (19:1). Its precise location is debated. Those scholars who seek a natural explanation for the smoke, fire, loud noise, and earthquake suggest that the mountain was an active volcano. But if the phenomena were all signs of God's supernatural intervention, then Mt. Sinai could be any number of places. Modern opinion leans toward Jebel Musa, part of a granite ridge that reaches 2,200 feet above the plain.[1] The rest of Exodus takes place at Mt. Sinai.

1. The covenant between God and Israel is a free gift to Israel in the sense that before Israel did anything, God saved the nation from slavery because of His free promise to Abraham. In

For Thought and Discussion:
a. According to 19:3-6, in what sense is the Lord the God of the Jews only?

b. In what sense is He the God of the whole earth?

For Thought and Discussion: Peter applies Exodus 19:6 to Christians (see 1 Peter 2:9). In what sense is the church the new Israel? What are some of the most important differences between Israel and the body of Christ?

Optional Application: How can you live as part of God's holy kingdom of priests? What specific acts will this involve during the coming week?

another sense, though, the covenant is conditional. What are the conditions and the promise (see 19:5-6)?

If _____

_____

_____

then_____

_____

_____

2. In your own words, explain what you think God means by . . .

"my treasured possession"_____

_____

_____

_____

"a kingdom of priests" _____

_____

_____

_____

"a holy nation" _____

_____

_____

_____

---

*A **kingdom of priests and a holy nation*** (19:6). A kingdom differs from just a group of people in that it has a king whom its citizens obey. Priests mediate between men and God and are set apart (made holy) from worldly pursuits in order to serve God fully. (See also the definition of "holy".)

3. What is Israel's response to God's message in 19:3-6 (see 19:7-8)?

_____

_____

_____

4. What does God command and do to impress upon Israel His utter holiness (see 19:10-25)?

_____

_____

_____

_____

_____

Abstain from sexual relations (19:15). Not because sex was sinful. Sex epitomized the physical, earthy side of man. To prepare for encounters with the holy, ancient people abstained for a time from all sorts of normal activities. This symbolized turning temporarily away from the commonplace and toward the holy. Abstaining from food, sex, and so on also helped a person concentrate fully on preparing himself inwardly.

The Ten Commandments (20:1-21)

Words (20:1). A technical term for "covenant stipulations" in the ancient Near East (as in 24:3,8; 34:28). The ten "words" in 20:2-17 are the basic stipulations of Israel's covenant with God.[2] They are "the original kernel of the *Torah* . . . around which the whole of the rest may be grouped as an expansion . . . The 'ten words' are at once the beginning and the heart of the Mosaic revelation."[3]

This passage is elsewhere called the "Ten Commandments" (Exodus 34:28; Deuteronomy 4:13; 10:4). From Greek we get the term *Decalogue*, which means literally "Ten Words."

For Thought and Discussion: Which of the Ten Commandments seem like moral principles common to most cultures? Which do not?

For Further Study: Compare Exodus 20:2-17 to Moses' restatement of the Decalogue in Deuteronomy 5:6-21, shortly before his death. What differences do you see?

99

For Further Study:
a. How does Christ explain the true meaning of each commandment in Matthew 5:17-48; 12:1-14; 15:1-9; 19:1-9?
b. How can you apply each teaching?

For Thought and Discussion: What gracious act is the basis of the Lord's right to be your King?

For Thought and Discussion: Does the first commandment imply that there are "other gods" (20:3)? Explain.

For Thought and Discussion: a. Why is it an offense against God to make a visible representation of Him?
b. Do you think 20:4 means God is "off limits" for the visual arts (painting, sculpture, and so on)? Why or why not?
c. How else can one make an idol of God other than with a physical object?

The Decalogue reflects the structure of royal treaties of Moses' day. It is worded like a covenant between a great king and a subject king or people: (1) The great king identifies himself in a preamble; then (2) he sketches his previous gracious acts that should have earned the gratitude of the subject(s); then (3) he states the treaty stipulations that the subject(s) must obey.[4]

5. What gracious act is the basis of the Lord's right to be Israel's King (20:2)?

_____

_____

No other gods before me (20:3). The preposition translated "before" or "besides" means literally, "to my face." "This slightly unusual phrase seems also to be used of taking a second wife while the first is alive . . . a breach of an exclusive personal relationship . . . It then links with the description of God as a 'jealous God' in verse 5 . . . The main thrust is clear: because of [the Lord's] nature and because of what [He] has done, He will not share His worship with another: He is unique."[5]

Misuse (20:7). "Take . . . in vain" in KJV and NASB. This includes taking an oath to do something in the Lord's name and not doing it, swearing false testimony in His name, profanity, and flippant use of "the Lord told me . . ."

6. What is one specific implication that 20:3-6 has for your life this week? (List more than one if you like.)

_____

_____

_____

100

7. Why did God command Israel to make one day in seven holy by not working on it (see 20:8-11)? (*Optional*: See also Exodus 23:12; 31:13-17; Deuteronomy 5:13-15.)

_____

_____

_____

8. How serious was God about the Sabbath? What indications do you find in 31:13-17; 34:21; 35:1-3?

_____

_____

_____

_____

9. Paul refers to the commandment to honor one's parents (see 20:12) as the first one "with a promise" (Ephesians 6:2). Why?

_____

_____

_____

10. How does an adult or a child "honor" his parents?

_____

_____

_____

11. What positive value does each of the sixth through ninth commandments reflect?

20:13 _____

20:14 _____

20:15 _____

20:16 _____

For Thought and Discussion: What contrast does 20:5-6 imply between the extent of God's grace and that of His wrath?

For Thought and Discussion: Why is it good news that God loves you jealously and won't share you with other gods (see 20:5)?

Optional Application: What "other gods" take you away from whole-hearted devotion to the Lord?

Optional Application: Do you misuse God's name in any way? If so, confess and ask God to work on this area of your life. Commit yourself to doing anything you can about this.

For Further Study: Study Jesus' teaching on the Sabbath in Luke 6:1-11.

For Thought and Discussion: How is the Sabbath law relevant to Christians?

For Further Study:
On the meaning
of the word *honor*
and other laws
about parents,
see Leviticus 19:3;
20:9; Deuteronomy
21:18-21; Psalm
91:15; Proverbs 4:8;
Matthew 15:1-9.

**For Thought and
Discussion:** How
does the last com-
mandment demon-
strate that the Law
of God deals with
the heart, not just
behavior?

**For Thought and
Discussion:** During
the revelation of the
Ten Commandments,
the people were
terrified. How does
true fear of the Lord
differ from what the
Israelites were feeling
(see 20:18-20)?

**Optional
Application:** Do the
Ten Commandments
seem like burdens
or blessings to you?
Read Psalm 19; 119;
and Romans 7:22. Ask
God to help you love
His Law.

12. Coveting (see 20:17) doesn't appear to do the
harm that murder, adultery, or theft does.
Why, then, is it included in God's ten chief
commandments?

_____

_____

_____

Your response

13. What one aspect of 19:1–20:21 would you like to
concentrate on for application?

_____

_____

_____

_____

14. How would you like this to affect the way you
think and live?

_____

_____

_____

_____

15. What action can you take to begin letting this
happen?

_____

_____

_____

16. List any questions you have about 19:1–20:21.

_____

_____

_____

For the group

Warm-up. Ask, "What gives God the right to tell you personally what to do?" Compare your answers to those you wrote for question 5.

Questions. Decide ahead of time which issue(s) you want to focus on from this packed passage. Choose a few discussion questions from the margins that will go to your group's heart, or concentrate on applying each of the Ten Commandments to your lives. If necessary, preface such a discussion by exploring how the New Testament tells Christians to treat these Old Testament commands (see the box below). Christians are "under grace," but Jesus Christ, Paul, and James all teach that the Ten Commandments summarize the love toward God and man that is our grateful response to grace.

Prayer. Praise God for His awesome holiness, revealed in fire and thunder on Mt. Sinai. Thank Him that you are free to approach His holiness because Jesus' blood consecrates you. Thank Him for the gracious gift of His Law. Ask Him to help each of you love and keep His commands this week, and to reveal Himself even more deeply.

For Further Study: Study in the Gospels what Jesus says about the Law.

Optional Application: Do you try to earn God's love and blessings by doing good things? Do you find it hard to trust Him to love you freely? Do you do good out of gratitude or self-interest?

The Purpose of the Law

The Lord established His covenant with Abraham and his descendants centuries before, and all He had done or would do was nothing but the fulfillment of that covenant. Because the Israelites were already God's people by virtue of that covenant, He liberated them from Egypt (see Exodus 1:17,20-21; 2:23-25; 3:7-10). Why, then, did God make another covenant (the Mosaic covenant) in addition to the one with Abraham?

This covenant was not absolutely new or independent, but was only a new phase of the Abrahamic covenant. It was necessary because now God's people were no longer a few individuals or a family, but an entire nation. Israel needed more extensive laws to govern its corporate life. One of the Law's purposes was like any code's aim: simply to restrain sinful people from uncontrolled wrongdoing. On a more positive note, it taught Israel to order its individual and social life according

(continued on page 104)

(continued from page 103)

to God's holy character. When people failed to fulfill it, it proved that even those who knew God's will would not and could not do it well enough to deserve His blessing. In all this, the Law's purpose was not to save Israel spiritually, but to train Israel to understand Christ when He came (see Galatians 3:19-25).

The New Testament shows several ways in which the Jews reacted to the Law. Some ignored it. Others manipulated it for their own earthly gain. Still others—truly religious people—tried to use it to gain merit in God's eyes because they couldn't imagine depending on His grace to give them love (see Luke 18:9-14). For others, God's absolute commands only intensified the moral and spiritual struggle in their hearts and highlighted the power of sin in their lives (see Romans 7:1-12).

These reactions to the Law influenced how the Jews reacted to Jesus and to the apostles. Those who were confident of their own ability to please God by keeping the Law were the ones who most bitterly opposed the gospel. Those who recognized the futility of attempts to win God's favor by keeping the Law were likely to see in Christ their only hope. The apostle Paul showed both attitudes at different times in his life (see Acts 22:3-5; 26:2-11; Galatians 1:11–2:21; Philippians 3:4-11).

Jesus' high value on the Law as God's will permeates the Gospels. His interpretations and applications were more rigorous than most other Jews' (see Matthew 5:17-48; 19:16-26; 22:34-40), but He stressed that God could save anyone who recognized his inability to satisfy God (see Luke 18:9-14,24-27). Paul emphasizes the impossibility of keeping the Law well enough to earn salvation *and* the importance of keeping it with God's help as a response to salvation (see Romans 13:8-10).

1. F. C. Fensham, "Mount Sinai," *New Bible Dictionary*, ed. J. D. Douglas et al. (Wheaton, IL: Tyndale, 1982), 1120.
2. Kenneth Barker, ed., *The NIV Study Bible* (Grand Rapids, MI: Zondervan, 1985), 115.
3. Brevard Childs, *The Book of Exodus* (Philadelphia: Westminster, 1974), 367.
4. Barker, 115.
5. R. A. Cole, *Exodus* (Downers Grove, IL: InterVarsity, 1973), 153–154.

LESSON TWELVE

EXODUS 20:22–23:19
Life Under God's Lordship

At Sinai, God reminded the Israelites of what He had done for them. But just as importantly, He revealed what they were to be to Him — a special treasure, a kingdom of priests, a holy nation. He proclaimed the Ten Words as the foundational principles for their nation. Then, to ensure that these lofty principles did not remain simply theory, He spelled out how they would be incarnated and incorporated into the people's everyday lives.

As you read 20:22–23:19, think about what God was revealing about Himself (His concerns, priorities, values) in these laws.

1. In the following outline, tell what subjects or areas of life are dealt with in each passage.

    20:22-26 _____

    21:1-11 _____

    21:12-36 _____

       21:12-27 _____

       21:28-32 _____

       21:33-36 _____

    22:1-15 _____

       22:1-4 _____

       22:5-6 _____

105

22:7-15 _____

22:16-31 _____

22:16-17_____

22:18-20 _____

22:21-27_____

22:28-31 _____

23:1-9 _____

23:10-12 _____

23:13-19 _____

These are the laws (21:1). Several passages in the Pentateuch list laws on various specific areas of life (see Exodus 20:22–23:19; 34:17-26; Leviticus 17:1–26:13; Deuteronomy 12:1–26:19). They are mostly applications of the Ten Commandments to specific situations, such as property rights, personal injuries, social justice, worshiping the Lord, and respecting authority. Exodus 20:22–23:19 is called "the Book of the Covenant" (24:7).

The laws in these codes are cast in two forms. One is simple and absolute ("Anyone who attacks his father or his mother must be put to death" — 21:15). The other is more complex and takes into account mitigating or aggravating circumstances (21:28-32 is an example of such "if . . ." laws).

On the relationship between Israel's law codes and those of other nations, see the box "Other Ancient Near Eastern Law Codes" (on pages 113 and 114).

Taken from my altar (21:14). In pagan countries, a person could claim refuge from pursuing avengers by holding onto the horns of an altar. It was forbidden to take a wrongdoer from the altar to punish him. This was practiced to some extent in Israel (see 1 Kings 1:50-51; 2:28), but the altar was no protection for a murderer. **Walk around outside with his staff** (21:19). "Is convalescing in a satisfactory way."[1]

106

Eye for eye (21:24). The point of this judicial principle is that punishment must fit the crime. The common standard of tribal justice in Moses' time was vengeance. If a man was killed, his kinsmen would try to kill the killer (and often his whole family). If a man was injured, his kinsmen would still try to kill the guilty person. This was unacceptable to God. Instead, He said that punishment must be neither more nor less than the crime deserved, and that it should be chosen to suit the kind of crime. "Eye for eye" was a figure of speech. Actual bodily mutilation rarely occurred in Israel; monetary fines were much more common. Both proportionate restitution and fines are basic to Western judicial tradition today.

God meant proportionate restitution to be a legal standard for regulating society. However, Jesus found people demanding strict justice, rather than granting love and mercy, from their neighbors in everyday dealings. This application of "eye for eye" He rebuked (see Matthew 5:38-42).

May redeem his life by the payment of (21:30). If the victim's family is willing to take money instead of demanding the man's death, he may pay them. However, the ransom is not to compensate the family for loss but to save the bull-owner's life. His life is forfeit because he caused a death.

Bride-price (22:16). A bridegroom normally paid a substantial sum to the bride's father as compensation for the loss of her labor and as insurance for her support if she was widowed.

Cloak (22:26). If a man had nothing but his cloak to give as collateral, then he was one of the poorest of the poor.

Festival (23:14). All Israelite men were required to attend the three annual festivals at the nation's central meeting place (see 23:15-17). *Unleavened Bread* was celebrated at the beginning of the religious year (the middle of the agricultural year) in March–April, at the time of the barley harvest. *Harvest* (or Firstfruits, or Weeks, later called Pentecost) was connected with the wheat harvest in

For Thought and Discussion: Why do you think Jesus told us to treat people with generosity rather than justice (see Matthew 5:38-42)? Do you think He was rejecting the principle of fair retribution for legal systems as well as private relationships? Why or why not?

For Further Study: Compare the usual price for a slave (see Exodus 21:32) to the price for which Judas sold Jesus (see Matthew 26:14-15).

May–June. ***Ingathering*** (or Tabernacles, or Booths) took place in September–October after the harvesting of orchards and vines (the end of the agricultural year).

Although all three were related to the agricultural cycle, they also commemorated saving acts in Israel's history. Unleavened Bread celebrated the deliverance from Egypt, as did Ingathering (see Leviticus 23:43). The Feast of Harvest later came to commemorate the giving of the Law at Sinai.[2]

Cook a young goat (23:19). The purpose of this command is obscure. However, archaeologists have uncovered an ancient Canaanite text that may prescribe cooking a kid in its mother's milk to enhance fertility. One writer theorizes, "The Canaanites thought that milk contained the seed of life, and they therefore sprinkled the ground with it. If a young goat was boiled in milk its vitality was doubled, and when this special milk was sprinkled on the ground one could even be more certain of its positive influence on the fertility of fields and plants."[3]

The translation of this text is debated, but an older theory is also possible. Milk represents life for an infant animal. The Law consistently separates holy from common, clean from unclean, and life from death. From this point of view, it would be scandalous to let the source of a young animal's life (milk) be the source of its death in cooking.[4] This principle of separation also makes sense of laws like Deuteronomy 22:9-11.

---

2. What do 20:22-26; 22:18-20,28-31; 23:14-19 say about God's priorities?

_____

_____

_____

_____

3. What seem to be the purposes of Israel's three annual festivals (see 23:14-17)?

108

_____

_____

_____

_____

4. In other Near Eastern cultures, a slave was the total, permanent property of his or her master. What humanitarian limits did God place on slavery in Israel (see 21:1-11,20-21,26-27)?

_____

_____

_____

_____

_____

5. How does God's Law stress the value of human life (see 21:12-32)?

_____

_____

_____

_____

_____

6. What is the point of having "if . . ." laws like 21:12-14,28-29; 22:2-3,14-15?

_____

_____

_____

_____

For Thought and Discussion:
a. Why was it unjust to free a female slave on her own in that culture (see 21:7-11)?
b. If a person had so many debts that he had to sell all his land, do you think it was unjust to have him sell six years of his labor to pay off his debts? Why or why not?

For Thought and Discussion: Are the punishments prescribed in these laws intended as revenge, remedial discipline, deterrent to others, or what? Give reasons for your view.

Optional Application: Ignorance and neglect were as punishable as deliberate infractions when they affected others (see 22:5-6,14). Have you damaged anyone's possessions or feelings because of carelessness? If so, what can you do about this?

For Thought and Discussion: What provisions in the code were intended to make sure that crime doesn't pay?

For Thought and Discussion: What do you think of the laws in 21:17 and 22:3?

For Further Study: See the principle of restitution (see Exodus 22:1-4) applied in Luke 19:8-10.

7. What attitudes toward one's own and others' property do you find in 21:33–22:15?

_____

_____

_____

_____

8. What limits does God put on the right to defend one's property, and why (see 22:2-3)?

_____

_____

_____

_____

9. Would you say that the laws in 20:22–23:19 are based on a realistic or an idealistic view of human nature? What gives you this impression?

_____

_____

_____

_____

_____

10. What does 22:21-27 tell you about God's character and priorities?

_____

_____

_____

_____

11. How does 23:4-5 illustrate the principle Jesus later expresses in Matthew 5:44?

_____

_____

_____

_____

12. Think about the purposes of the Sabbath year and Sabbath day (see 23:10-12). What do they say about God's character and priorities?

_____

_____

_____

_____

13. Summarize what the Book of the Covenant (see 20:22–23:19) tells you about God.

_____

_____

_____

_____

_____

_____

Your response

14. What one insight from this lesson seems most personally relevant to you?

_____

_____

_____

_____

15. How would you like to see your life affected by this truth?

_____

_____

For Thought and Discussion: Why was the penalty for cursing sometimes as severe as for actual killing (see Exodus 21:15,17)? See also Matthew 5:21-22; 12:34.

Optional Application: Have you committed any wrongs that require restitution?

Christians are no longer "under law" (Romans 6:15), but we are "slaves to God" (Romans 6:22). How, then, are passages like Exodus 20:22–23:19 relevant to our lives?

_____

_____

_____

_____

16. What can you do about this?

_____

_____

_____

_____

17. List any questions you have about 20:22–23:19.

_____

_____

_____

For the group

Warm-up. Ask, "After a week of focusing on the Ten Commandments and another week looking at the Book of the Covenant, how are you feeling about your own ability to obey God? Do you feel like you could live up to His expectations if you tried? Why or why not?" The main reasons for Christians to study the laws of Exodus are (1) to learn what God values and what He desires of His people; (2) to be convicted of how far we fall short of God's standards; and (3) to see what habits and attitudes God desires to instill in us by grace and the power of His Spirit. This warm-up should tell you how well (2) is being accomplished in the hearts of your group members. Encourage everyone to be honest. Ask people to share what happened when they tried to apply the Ten Commandments this week. Some people actually feel they get worse when they work on obeying God; this usually means that they are just more aware of their rebelliousness than before.

Questions. Question 1 is just background observations; you don't need to discuss it in detail. The rest of the questions deal with the motives and attitudes behind the laws. You may feel that Israel's laws are not literally applicable to your lives, but that God's character, values, and priorities are unchanging. Come to some conclusions about what these chapters demand of each of you. This should not be a brief wallowing in guilt, nor a determination to work and strive to keep the laws by your own strength, but a humble commitment to seek God's grace to do what you hear Him telling you to do.

Prayer. Praise God for the compassion and justice He reveals through His Law. Thank Him for being concerned with even the details of the daily lives of the most ordinary people. Ask Him to build His character into you, so that you value life and people as much as He does, and so that you show these values in practical, everyday ways. Confess any ways in which you have violated His values and not repented.

Other Ancient Near Eastern Law Codes

Moses said, "What other nation is so great as to have such righteous decrees and laws as this body of laws I am setting before you today?" (Deuteronomy 4:8). A comparison with other Near Eastern nations shows that Moses spoke truly.

In centuries of history, Egypt never had a law code that gave predictable, consistent guidelines for rights, duties, and penalties. Indeed, the Egyptian language had no word for "law." The Pharaoh was regarded as a god on earth, whose every decree supposedly embodied truth and justice. It didn't matter whether people were treated alike or in proportion to their deeds. In the same way, the petty kings of Canaan and Syria decided justice by their personal whims, not by permanent laws.

We know of several Babylonian law codes, but none of these stated what judges were supposed to do. They recorded only what some judges had done in the past, so that a judge might use a case as a guide if he chose to do so.

(continued on page 114)

113

(continued from page 113)

Assyria, likewise, compiled past decisions but left judges free to judge by their opinions.[5]

No other code than Israel's included religious law or claimed that a god gave it or was its authority for justice. No other code gave motives or reasons for its decisions, as in Exodus 20:5 and 23:8-9. Israel's Law commanded the death penalty for crimes against God and against the holiness of life, but it was strikingly humane compared to other codes. Only Deuteronomy 25:11-12 mentions bodily mutilation, in contrast to many places in Babylonian, Hittite, and other codes. Flogging was limited to forty lashes in Israel (see Deuteronomy 25:3).

Other codes treated commoners' lives as less valuable than noblemen's. They regarded harm done to a woman, a slave, or an ox all as harm to a man's property. For instance, if a nobleman caused the death of a noblewoman, Hammurabi's code said that the killer's *daughter* had to die. If a nobleman caused a slavewoman's death, he paid one-third of a mine of silver to her owner.[6] By contrast, Israel's law protected women and slaves explicitly from being used as property and made justice the same for all social classes. Physical discipline of slaves was limited, though not forbidden (see Exodus 21:20-21,26-27), and killing a slave was punished the same way as killing a freeman.

1. Kenneth Barker, ed., *The NIV Study Bible* (Grand Rapids, MI: Zondervan, 1985), 117.
2. R. A. Cole, *Exodus* (Downers Grove, IL: InterVarsity, 1973), 179.
3. W. H. Gispen, *Exodus* (Grand Rapids, MI: Zondervan, 1982), 232.
4. Jacob Milgrom, "You Shall Not Boil a Kid in Its Mother's Milk," *Bible Review*, vol. 1, no. 3 (Washington, D. C.: Biblical Archaeology Society, Fall 1985): 48–55.
5. Roland de Vaux, *Ancient Israel: Volume 1: Social Institutions* (New York: McGraw-Hill, 1965), 144–150.
6. Gordon Fee and Douglas Stuart, *How to Read the Bible for All Its Worth* (Grand Rapids, MI: Zondervan, 1982), 144.

EXODUS 23:20–24:18

Covenant Confirmed

If God's commands covered all of life, so did His care. While the people trembled at the foot of Mt. Sinai, Moses climbed it (see 20:18-21) to receive the Ten Commandments (see 20:1-17) and the Book of the Covenant (see 20:22–23:19). Now, having revealed how His people must live, the Lord promises to lead them to the land He has prepared for them. When Israel accepts God's terms, the covenant is ratified, and Moses returns to speak with the Lord. Read 23:20–24:18.

Promises and instructions (23:20-33)

1. God promises to send an angel with His Name (His character, the authority to represent His presence). What will this angel do (see 23:20-23,27-28)?

   _____

   _____

   _____

   _____

   _____

2. How must Israel respond in order for the angel to fulfill his mission (see 23:21-22)?

_____

_____

_____

_____

_____

Rebellion (23:21). "The fundamental idea . . . is a breach of relationships, civil or religious, between two parties." The word was used primarily for rebellion against rulers. "By analogy . . . Israel was accused of rebelling against her divine king and the established covenant between them (see Isaiah 1:28; 48:8; Ezekiel 2:3; Hosea 8:1) . . . The term [*rebellion*] is a collective which denotes the sum of misdeeds and a fractured relationship."[1]

---

3. While God promised to clear Canaan of its inhabitants, what task did He charge Israel to complete (see 23:23-24,31-33)?

_____

_____

_____

_____

4. What other specific benefits would the Israelites experience as a result of obeying the Lord (see 23:25-26)?

_____

_____

_____

_____

116

5. Why couldn't God drive out all of Israel's enemies at once (see 23:29-30)?

_____

_____

_____

_____

Borders (23:31). The Old Testament describes the Promised Land in two ways. In passages like 23:23, it is identified as the land of certain peoples whom Israel must destroy. In those like 23:31, it is indicated in general terms by its boundaries. The location of the Promised Land was certain, but its precise extent depended on Israel's faith and commitment to take possession of it. In Joshua and Judges, we find that Israel failed to inherit as much as it might have because of sin and faithlessness. Eventually, the people's unfaithfulness to the covenant led them to forfeit their right to live as an independent state, and they were forced to submit to foreign domination (see 2 Kings 17; Jeremiah 25).[2]

For Thought and Discussion: How many times in 23:20-33 does the Lord refer to His actions on Israel's behalf, and how many references are there to what Israel must do? What does this indicate about the Lord's concern for and relationship to His people?

6. Was Israel's greatest danger physical or moral? Explain.

_____

_____

_____

_____

7. How did God instruct the nation to avoid this danger?

_____

_____

_____

_____

117

Optional Application:
a. Compare Exodus 23:32-33 to 2 Corinthians 6:14–7:1. What is God's consistent will here? Why does He object to covenants (close ties) between His people and idolaters?

b. Are any human relationships in your life right now menacing your faithfulness to God? If so, what should you do about this?

For Further Study:
Read in Hebrews 9:19-28 an explanation of the blood covenant in Exodus 24.

8. How is 23:20-33 relevant to Christians? In what ways are God's promises and commands for Christians similar?

_____

_____

_____

_____

_____

_____

_____

_____

Covenant ratified (24:1-18)

9. How does Moses act as mediator between God and Israel in 24:1-18?

_____

_____

_____

_____

_____

10. In chapter 19, only Moses even got to touch the mountain. Whom does the Lord call somewhat nearer in chapter 24 (see 24:1)?

_____

_____

_____

_____

118

11. What is the Lord teaching Israel about Himself through His instructions in 24:1-2?

_____

_____

_____

_____

_____

For Further Study: Compare Exodus 24:10 to Isaiah 6:1-4 and Ezekiel 1:4-28.

Seventy of the elders of Israel (24:1). This figure corresponds to the number of those who went into Egypt with Jacob (see 1:5). These may have been the men Moses selected on his father-in-law's advice (see 18:17-26), but the text does not say so. In any case, "elders"—heads of families and tribes—had long been Israel's leaders (see 3:16). They were responsible for judging disputes (see Deuteronomy 22:13-19), military leadership (see Joshua 8:10), and counsel (see 1 Samuel 4:3).

Blood (24:6,8). "The blood on the altar symbolizes God's forgiveness and his acceptance of the offering; the blood on the people points to an oath that binds them in obedience."[3] The blood gives tangible expression that this commitment is sacred and serious. To break faith after being sprinkled with the sacrificial blood would mean incurring bloodguilt (equivalent to murder) and God's disciplinary judgment.

Book (24:7). The blood of the covenant was one of the crucial elements of Israel's faith. The Book of the Covenant was the other crucial element. While God was hidden from man's gaze (but see 24:9-11), He made the knowledge of His will permanently available so that His people might obey and please Him.

Ate and drank (24:11). A meal to cement the covenant between God and Israel, like the one that sealed the covenant between Israel and Jethro (see 18:12). Meals were often used to express the bond of fellowship between a god and his devotees

For Thought and Discussion: Why do you think the Lord used dramatic natural phenomena (see 24:17) and a long period of time (see 24:18) when He revealed His laws to Moses for Israel? How does this compare to the way He revealed Himself through Christ, as portrayed in the Gospels?

in the ancient world. (That is part of the point of the Passover meal.)

Tablets of stone (24:12). God inscribed the Ten Commandments on each of these (see 31:18). It was customary in the ancient Near East to make two copies of a covenant document, one for each party. Each party usually put his copy in the presence of his god. Therefore, both copies of Israel's covenant with the Lord were kept in the ark of the covenant (see 25:21) in the Lord's royal tent. God probably inscribed the document on stone in order to demonstrate its divine origin and permanence.

12. Describe the ceremony by which God and Israel confirmed their covenant (see 24:4-11).

_____

_____

_____

_____

13. Read 1 Corinthians 11:23-26. How was the ratification of the New Covenant like that of the Old Covenant in Exodus? How does Exodus help you understand what Jesus did?

_____

_____

_____

_____

_____

Your response

14. What insight from 23:20–24:18 would you like to take to heart this week?

120

_____

_____

_____

_____

15. How would you like to grow in this area?

_____

_____

_____

_____

_____

16. What steps can you take to cooperate with God in accomplishing this?

_____

_____

_____

_____

_____

17. List any questions you have about 23:20–24:18.

_____

_____

_____

_____

Meditate on the cost Christ paid to ratify your covenant with God. How can you take that covenant seriously this week? How can you do what 23:21,24-25,32-33 describes? Plan daily time this week to *listen* to God's instructions, then *do* what He says.

For the group

Warm-up. Ask group members to share briefly how God has been active in their lives during the past week.

Questions. One issue you may need to deal with is to what extent we can "claim" Old Testament promises like 23:22,25-27. If you decide that you can claim such promises, take seriously the conditions that go along with them (pay attention to God's messenger, don't rebel, listen to the Lord, worship Him, obey Him, smash idols, don't make covenants with the wicked, and so on). How can each of you actively seek to obey such commands during the coming week?

Prayer. Thank God for sealing the New Covenant in the blood of Jesus, for making Christ's death and resurrection a sign that you and He are committed to each other. Thank Him for all His promises to you. Ask Him to enable you to take your covenant seriously in worship, love, and obedience. If appropriate, consider celebrating the Lord's Supper together as a sign of your communion with Him in the New Covenant and a proclamation of His death and resurrection.

1. C. H. Livingston, "rebellion," in *Theological Wordbook of the Old Testament*, vol. 2, ed. R. L. Harris, et al. (Chicago: Moody, 1980), 741.
2. For a discussion of the boundaries of the Promised Land as presented in the Old Testament, see Barry J. Beitzel, *The Moody Atlas of Bible Lands* (Chicago: Moody, 1985), 8–13.
3. Kenneth Barker, ed., *The NIV Study Bible* (Grand Rapids, MI: Zondervan, 1985), 122.

EXODUS 25:1–27:21; 30:1–31:18

The Tabernacle: Its Specifications

Israelite religion was not just a matter of commandments. In chapters 25 through 31, the Lord details His desire to live in the midst of His people, and His concern that they not only obey His commands, but even more that they enjoy communion with Him.
Read 25:1–27:21 and 30:1–31:18.

Optional Application: How should God's indwelling presence affect your priorities and actions this week?

1. What was the purpose of the tabernacle (see 25:8)?

_____

_____

_____

Sanctuary . . . tabernacle (25:8-9). Literally, "holy place" and "dwelling place." Before Israel became a nation, God communed mainly with individuals and families (see Genesis 6:8; 12:1-3; 26:2-5; 28:13-15). Now He shows that His concern is not only for the privileged few, but for an entire people through whom He plans to bless all mankind (see Genesis 12:3).
  The Old Testament progressively develops the theme of God in the midst of His people. The birth of Christ, however, marked the beginning of the final phase. The gospel of John says literally that "the Word became flesh and [*tabernacled*] among us" (John 1:14).

123

For Further Study:
Trace the principle of
voluntary offerings
(see 2 Chronicles 24:8-
14; 1 Corinthians 16:2;
2 Corinthians 8:1–9:15).
Why is voluntary giv-
ing so important?

**Optional
Application:**
Read Luke 21:1-4;
2 Corinthians 9:7. Do
you tend to be rejoic-
ing or reluctant when
you give?

**For Thought and
Discussion:** Is the
worship of God now a
strictly spiritual mat-
ter, or does it neces-
sarily involve physical
and material accesso-
ries? Why?

2. During His incarnation, Jesus fulfilled God's
   promise to tabernacle or dwell with His people.
   How is He dwelling among His people now?

   Matthew 18:20 _____

   _____

   John 14:16-17 _____

   _____

   John 14:23 _____

   _____

3. What will be the crowning feature of the new
   order God will establish at the end of time
   (see Revelation 21:1-4)?

   _____

   _____

   _____

4. How were the tabernacle and its furnishings to
   be financed (see Exodus 25:2-7; 30:11-16)?

   _____

   _____

   _____

5. Why did each Israelite owe a ransom to the
   Lord for his life?

   _____

   _____

   _____

6. What does each of these offerings say about
   each person's responsibility and relationship to
   the Lord?

   _____

   _____

   _____

Offerings (25:3). *Blue, purple and scarlet* (25:4) were royal colors, because the dyes were extremely expensive (they came from shellfish and the eggs and carcasses of a special kind of worm).[1]

Fine linen was high-quality cloth. Egyptian samples have been found that were woven so tightly that they cannot be distinguished from silk without a magnifying glass.[2]

Goat hair—the hair of long-haired black goats was often used to weave cloth for tents.

Ram skins dyed red (25:5). "After all the wool had been removed from the skins. The final product was similar to present-day morocco leather."[3]

Acacia wood ("shittim" in KJV) "is darker and harder than oak and is avoided by wood-eating insects. It is common in the Sinai peninsula."[4]

Ark (25:10). This Hebrew word means "chest," but is a different word from the one for Noah's ark and the reed basket in which the infant Moses was placed (see 2:3). The ark is mentioned first probably because it represented the Lord's throne in the midst of His people (see 1 Samuel 4:4; 2 Samuel 6:2).

Pure gold (25:11). The furnishings within the tabernacle itself were all of "pure gold," considered a perfect, royal metal uncontaminated by silver or other impurities. Even the frame of the tent was covered with gold (see 26:29). But beginning with the bases of the tabernacle's outer curtain, the furnishings outside the holy tent (see 26:36-37; 27:1-7; 30:17-21) were of bronze. This is a harder metal, more suited for heavy use. It is also an alloy, so it is by definition not pure. Its association with blood sacrifice and cleansing, as well as later uses, imply some symbolism of judgment for sin. The bases that supported the whole structure were of silver (see 26:19,21,25,32) made from the money that ransomed each firstborn male Israelite.

Atonement (25:17). The word comes from the verb, "to cover." When a sacrifice "atoned for" or

For Thought and Discussion: Paul speaks of believers individually and corporately as God's temple (see 1 Corinthians 6:12-20; Ephesians 2:19-22). How does the description of the tabernacle and its furnishings enrich your appreciation of what it means to be God's holy dwelling?

125

Optional Application: Is worship at the center of your life as the tabernacle was in the center of Israel's encampment? How can you build it into each day and prepare yourself physically and spiritually for worship?

"covered" a sin, the sin was paid for and so was covered from God's sight. Atonement is the act of divine grace by which God reconciles sinful people to Himself. In the Old Testament, the shed blood of a sacrifice atoned for sin; the animal paid the death penalty on the sinner's behalf (see Leviticus 17:11). In the New Testament, Christ's shed blood does the same thing (see Romans 3:25; 1 John 2:2).

The lid of the ark, God's throne, was called the "atonement cover" or "mercy seat" (KJV). Once each year, the high priest sacrificed a special sin offering and took its blood into the Most Holy Place where the ark stood. He would sprinkle the blood on the atonement cover to make atonement for the people's sins so that the tabernacle would stay holy and the Lord would remain among His people.

7. The atonement cover or mercy seat was the lid of the ark. What was the purpose of the atonement cover (see Exodus 25:22)?

_____

_____

_____

Cherubim (25:18). "Probably similar to the carvings of winged sphinxes that adorned the armrests of royal thrones . . . in many parts of the Near East."[5] These cherubim flanked the Lord's throne like royal attendants, their wings shielding the area where the Lord's presence was manifested.

Bread of the Presence (25:30). "Showbread" in KJV. Twelve loaves were placed each week in the Holy Place of the tabernacle as a thank offering for the provision of daily bread, consecrating the fruit of Israel's labors. "Presence" refers to God's presence as provider and Lord.

Seven (25:37). This number often symbolizes completeness or perfection in the Bible.

8. The lampstand (see 26:31-40) gave the only light in the Holy Place. The Most Holy Place was lit only by the Lord's glory itself. The people were commanded to provide oil for the seven lamps so that they would never go out at night (see 27:20-21). Besides its practical function, what might the lampstand have symbolized?

_____

_____

_____

For Thought and Discussion: Israel's worship involved all the senses: sight, sound, touch, even the taste of sacrifice and the smell of incense. Should this be true of our worship? Why or why not?

For Thought and Discussion: What about God might the table for the Bread of the Presence indicate (see 25:23-30)?

Tabernacle (26:1-37). The Lord's royal tent was approximately 45 feet long by 15 feet wide by 15 feet high. It consisted of a sectionalized wooden framework covered by four layers of material (embroidered linen on the inside, then woven goat hair, then ramekin leather, then sea cow hide). On the inside it was divided into two compartments: the Holy Place (about 30 by 15 feet) and the Most Holy Place (about 15 by 15 feet). The Most Holy Place was a perfect cube.

The tabernacle was erected on the west side of a surrounding courtyard measuring about 150 by 75 feet. All around this courtyard, except for an entryway on the eastern side, was a curtain almost eight feet high.

9. Two different altars were to be made. How did these compare in size, material used, location, and purpose?

27:1-8 _____

_____

_____

30:1-10 _____

_____

_____

127

For Thought and Discussion: Why do you think God kept repeating that everything must be done according to the pattern He revealed (see 25:9,40; 26:30)?

For Thought and Discussion: a. What was the point of the Sabbath, according to 31:12-17?
    b. What indicates the seriousness with which Israel was to regard the Sabbath (see 31:14-15)?
    c. Why do you think the Lord kept repeating this instruction about the Sabbath?

Incense (30:1). "Its fragrant smoke symbolized the prayers of God's people" (see Psalm 141:2; Luke 1:10; Revelation 5:8; 8:3-4).[6]

Bronze basin (30:18). Made from bronze mirrors given by the Israelite women (see 38:8). (Glass mirrors were unknown at the time.)

Salted (30:35). Because salt never breaks down, it represented purity and faithfulness.

10. a. For what was the bronze basin ("laver" in KJV) used (see 30:17-21)?

_____

_____

_____

    b. What do you think was the spiritual significance of this?

_____

_____

_____

11. What was the Holy Spirit's role in the construction of the tabernacle (see 31:1-11)?

_____

_____

_____

_____

12. Hebrews 8:5 explains that the "pattern" (Exodus 25:40) God gave Moses for the earthly tabernacle was copied from the real dwelling place of God in heaven, the real tabernacle Christ entered to perform the final atoning sacrifice. What aspects of Christ's work are foreshadowed in each of the following?

    the ark (God's throne) with the atonement cover (*Optional*: See Hebrews 9:11-14; 1 John 2:2.)

_____

_____

_____

the table with the Bread of the Presence
(*Optional*: See John 6:48-51.)

_____

_____

_____

the lampstand (*Optional*: See John 8:12;
Matthew 5:14.)

_____

_____

_____

_____

the bronze altar of burnt offering (*Optional*: See
Hebrews 9:22.)

_____

_____

_____

the altar of incense (*Optional*: See Hebrews
7:25; Revelation 8:3.)

_____

_____

_____

the bronze basin for washing the priests
(*Optional*: See John 13:1-11; Hebrews 10:19-23.)

_____

_____

_____

For Further Study:
Study carefully what Hebrews 8:1–10:18 says about the tabernacle and its worship. Note especially the contrasts between the access to God under the Old Covenant and our privileges under the New Covenant.

**Optional
Application:**
Meditate this week on
what Christ accom-
plished for you in the
heavenly tabernacle
and on how He lived
out the symbolism of
each of the tent's fur-
nishings. Thank Him,
and respond with
worship and grateful
action.

the whole tent

_____

_____

_____

Your response

13. What insight from 25:1–27:21 or 30:1–31:18
    seems most relevant to your life, and how is it
    relevant?

    _____

    _____

    _____

    _____

14. What would you like to do in response?

    _____

    _____

    _____

15. List any questions you have about this lesson.

    _____

    _____

    _____

For the group

Warm-up. Ask, "When you gather with other believers
to worship God, is it easy for you to be caught up in
adoring God's majesty, or do you find worship hard?"
This question may catch the group by surprise, since
many of us associate being caught up in adoration

with emotional hype. Take a couple of minutes for group members to share their feelings about worship. Does it mean a lot to you, or not much? Why?

Questions. The goal of your discussion should be to get a sense of what God was trying to teach and accomplish by the way the tabernacle was made. Focus on the symbolism of each aspect and how it foreshadowed Christ. If possible, bring a study Bible, Bible handbook, or Bible dictionary with pictures of the tabernacle and its furnishings.

Several optional questions ask you how Christian worship should be like and unlike Israel's. If you want to explore this, start by asking what "worship" is. What is the goal of worship? How can your worship be "in the Spirit and in truth" (John 4:24), neither dry nor hyper-emotional?

Prayer. Thank God that although He is holy and unapproachable by corrupt humans, He has devised a way to dwell in the midst of His people. Praise Him for the way He accomplished this through Christ. Ask Him to enable you to draw near to Him in adoration.

The Significance of the Tabernacle

Eight characteristics of the tabernacle seem to have been meant to teach Israel important lessons:

1. There was only one central sanctuary, not many. This declared that the authorized approach to God was one, not many, and stressed Israel's spiritual unity.

2. The tabernacle stood at the center of Israel's encampment. This expressed that the nation's life must revolve around the Lord, and that He was dwelling in its midst for worship and fellowship.

3. Access to the tabernacle was limited. Only the priests could enter the sanctuary. Only the high priest could enter the Most Holy Place, and that only once a year with a sacrifice for sin. God sought intimate fellowship with His people, but He was still transcendent, still to be feared, still too holy to be approached by sin-stained humans.

4. Precious materials and artistry spoke of God's excellence. The Great King of Israel

(continued on page 132)

131

(continued from page 131)
deserved nothing less than the best men could offer.

5. The tabernacle was of modest proportions. Even the whole complex was microscopic in comparison with the temples and pyramids of Egypt (which covered acres). If quality counted, mere quantity did not. God was not interested in overwhelming His people into obedience, nor in being an overbearing presence in their lives. He didn't need to make bombastic claims to grandeur like Egypt's arrogant pharaohs.

6. Although the tabernacle was made of costly materials, it was fragile and required constant, loving care. A stone temple could withstand almost anything, but the tabernacle would survive only if faithfully maintained. What better way to illustrate that only as Israel cultivated her relationship with the Lord would she be able to enjoy fellowship with Him?

7. The tabernacle was portable. Even though God was leading His people to a permanent home, He wanted a portable dwelling to teach them that even in the Promised Land they would in some sense still be pilgrims and strangers (see Leviticus 25:23). The portable tabernacle reminded Israel that Abraham sought a "city with foundations, whose architect and builder is God" (Hebrews 11:10).

8. The tabernacle and its furnishings were planned by God, realized through divine enablement, and inhabited by the glory of the Lord. Israel's religion was from beginning to end God's creation, not man's.

1. Kenneth Barker, ed., *The NIV Study Bible* (Grand Rapids, MI: Zondervan, 1985), 122–123.
2. Barker, 123.
3. Barker, 123.
4. Barker, 123.
5. Barker, 123.
6. Barker, 131. For a more extensive discussion of the tabernacle, see D. W. Gooding, "Tabernacle," *The New Bible Dictionary*, 2nd ed., ed. J. D. Douglas, et. al. (Wheaton, IL: Tyndale, 1982), 1157–1160, and C. L. Feinberg, "Tabernacle," *Zondervan's Pictorial Encyclopedia of the Bible,* vol. 5, ed. Merrill C. Tenney (Grand Rapids, MI: Zondervan, 1975), 572–583.

EXODUS 28:1–29:46

The Tabernacle: Its Servants and Sacrifices

As He described the royal tent in which He would dwell among His people, the Lord also revealed who was to serve Him on Israel's behalf. Read 28:1–29:46.

1. Whom did God select to serve as priests, and to what tribe did they belong (see 4:14; 28:1)?

_____

_____

_____

Recall from the note "redeem" that the Levites were taken as the ransom price for the rest of the Israelites.

For Thought and Discussion: While the Lord said that all Israel was to be "a kingdom of priests and a holy nation" (19:6), He also created a formal priesthood in Israel. How does this compare with the situation in the body of Christ, and why?

Ephod (28:6). A sleeveless garment. Its front and back panels were fastened at the shoulders with two engraved onyx stones and tied at the waist with a waistband.

Urim and Thummim (28:30). These Hebrew words probably mean "the curses and the perfections." *Urim* begins with the first letter of the Hebrew alphabet, and *Thummim* with the last. The *Urim* and *Thummim* were sacred lots used somehow to determine God's will (see Numbers 27:21). Possibly, if *Urim* ("curses") dominated

For Thought and Discussion:
a. What was Moses' role in 28:1–29:46?
b. How does this contribute to the picture of Moses that is presented throughout Exodus?

For Further Study:
What elements from Exodus 25–31 can you find in the book of Revelation (see 21:5-21, for example).

For Further Study:
The Old Testament speaks of another priesthood, that of Melchizedek (see Genesis 14:17-20; Psalm 110:4). Read how Hebrews 4:14–7:28 bases on these verses the superiority of Christ's priesthood to Aaron's.

when the lots were cast, then the answer was "no," and if *Thummim* ("perfections") dominated, then the answer was "yes." It was believed that God controlled the outcome of casting lots (see Proverbs 16:33).[1]

___

2. What was the chief purpose of the rich and striking garments made for the priests (see Exodus 28:2,40)?

_____

_____

_____

_____

_____

3. Why did the high priest wear onyx stones on his shoulders engraved with the names of the twelve tribes of Israel (see 28:9-12)? What did this represent?

_____

_____

_____

_____

_____

4. Why did Aaron wear twelve stones with the names of the tribes on the "breastpiece for making decisions" (28:15-21,29)?

_____

_____

_____

_____

_____

5. What does God's provision of the *Urim* and *Thummim* say about Him?

134

_____

_____

_____

_____

_____

6. What did the engraved plate on Aaron's forehead symbolize (see 28:36-38)?

_____

_____

_____

_____

7. Jesus is our High Priest (see Hebrews 4:14).
What do you learn about His work from the
description of the high priest in Exodus 28:1-43?

_____

_____

_____

_____

8. Before Aaron and his sons could begin their
ministry as priests, what rites of consecration
were to be performed (see 29:1-37)? Describe
them in general.

_____

_____

_____

_____

_____

_____

**Optional
Application:**
   a. What do the
instructions for the
priests tell you about
what is involved in
ministry on behalf of
others?
   b. Are you will-
ing to devote the
same amount of time
and effort that was
demanded of Aaron
to meet others' spiri-
tual needs?
   c. How can you
act as a priest of the
Lord this week?

For Further Study:
On Jesus our High
Priest, read Hebrews
4:14–5:10; 6:13–8:13.

For Thought and Discussion: How does Israel's sacrificial system help you understand why the Lord's Supper is called *communion* ("fellowship") and *the Eucharist* ("thanksgiving")?

For Further Study: On the possibility of suffering judgment while serving as priest (found in Exodus 28:35), see Leviticus 10:1-20.

9. What was all of this designed to make possible (see 29:38-46)?

_____

_____

_____

_____

10. Read the box "Old Testament Sacrifice." What do you learn about Christ's work from Israel's sacrificial system?

    a. Why was Jesus crucified outside Jerusalem, away from consecrated ground (see Hebrews 13:11-13)?

    _____

    _____

    _____

    _____

    b. What was Jesus alluding to in calling the bread and wine of the Lord's Supper His body and blood (see Matthew 26:26-28)?

    _____

    _____

    _____

    _____

11. How did God demonstrate the enormous responsibility that was on His priests (see 28:31-33; 30:17-21)?

    _____

    _____

    _____

12. When meat was consecrated (made holy, set apart), it could no longer be eaten as common meat (see 29:31-34). The same was true of the tabernacle utensils. The formulas for the anointing oil and incense could not be used for everyday purposes (see 30:22-38). Why do you think God made such a sharp, utter distinction between the holy and the common?

_____

_____

_____

_____

_____

Your response

13. What aspect of 28:1–29:46 seems most relevant to your life, and how is it relevant?

_____

_____

_____

_____

_____

14. How would you like to respond to this truth in prayer and action?

_____

_____

_____

_____

For Thought and Discussion:
a. After their inaugural consecration, how often were the priests to wash themselves with water from the bronze laver (see 30:17-21)?
b. What parallels do you see between this and John 13:1-11?
c. How is this relevant to you?

For Thought and Discussion: Why do you think only priests could eat certain parts of the sacrificial meat (see 29:32-34)?

15. List any questions you have about 28:1–29:46.

_____

_____

_____

_____

For the group

Warm-up. Ask group members to tell what "holiness" means to them. What feelings and images come to mind when you think of holiness? Exodus is full of sights, sounds, and smells to impress the idea of holiness on Israel.

Questions. As in the last lesson, your goal should be to see how Israel's priesthood and sacrifices illuminate Christ's work. How did He act as priest for you? How can you act as priests in the world now?

Prayer. Thank God for instituting priests to stand before God on men's behalf and for instituting sacrifices to remove sin and restore fellowship. Ask Him to impress the implications of sin, atonement, and holiness on your hearts.

Old Testament Sacrifice

The sacrifices involved with the consecration of the priests (see 29:1-46) followed the standard progression of Israel's sacrifices. The basic principles behind the system were *substitution* and *satisfaction*; an animal died in place of the sinful person in order to restore fellowship between the person and God. The animal bore the death penalty for the person. These were the main kinds of sacrifices:

The sin offering (29:10-14) involved the sacrifice of a young bull. The men laid their hands on it to transfer their sin to it and claim it as their substitute. Its blood and vital organs were offered on the altar, while the rest of the carcass was burned outside the camp because it was

(continued on page 139)

138

(continued from page 138)
made unclean by bearing the men's sin. (In other situations, the sin offering was required to atone for specific sins a person committed.)

The burnt offering, a ram (29:15-18), was entirely consumed by fire on the altar. This atoned for unintentional sin in general, the sinful natures men were born with. It was wholly consumed because it expressed "devotion, commitment, and complete surrender to God."[2]

The wave offering (29:19-26) included another ram and several kinds of bread. This ram's blood was sprinkled on the priests as well as the altar. The animal and bread were burned only after Aaron and his sons waved or elevated portions of it in the Lord's presence. The wave offering thanked God for His goodness and provisions.

One breast of this second ram was granted to the priests as their portion and eaten by them (see 29:27-28). Thus, this sacrifice was also a *fellowship offering* ("peace offering" in KJV), the kind of sacrifice in which the worshipers ate a part. The fellowship offering was a communal meal to celebrate and give thanks for peace and fellowship between the worshipers and God.

Finally, burnt offerings were offered morning and evening each day thereafter (see 29:42-43) to signify that the nation daily rededicated itself to the Lord. Notice the order: sin offering (confession and atonement for specific sins), burnt offering (atonement for sinful human nature and personal surrender to the Lord), wave offering (thanks for blessings), fellowship offering (communion between God and man possible because sin is dealt with).

1. Kenneth Barker, ed., *The NIV Study Bible* (Grand Rapids, MI: Zondervan, 1985), 129.
2. Barker, 150.

EXODUS 32:1–33:6

Idolatry and Intercession

While Moses was on the mountain receiving instructions for Israel's worship, the people below were getting restless. Marching through the desert had been exhausting, but for more than a month the fugitives had been idle, waiting for Moses to reappear. Was he dead? Not knowing that Moses was even now getting a blueprint for worship based on the model of heaven itself, the Israelites decided to entertain themselves with the kind of worship they were used to. Read 32:1–33:6.

For Further Study:
On Israel's apostasy, see Deuteronomy 9:7-21; Psalm 106:19-23; 1 Corinthians 10:1-13.

1. In what ways do the words in 32:1 violate what God recently told Israel in the following verses?

   20:2 _____

   _____

   _____

   20:3 _____

   _____

   _____

   20:4 _____

   _____

   _____

   _____

For Thought and Discussion: Why do you think people are so prone to making idols?

For Further Study: Compare the golden calf incident in Exodus with 1 Kings 12:25-33.

2. What needs and desires do you think motivated Israel to request manufactured gods?

_____

_____

_____

_____

_____

3. The gold for the calf came from the plunder God had told the people to bring from their Egyptian neighbors (see 11:2-3; 12:35-36). What was this gold supposed to be used for (see 25:2-9)?

_____

_____

Cast in the shape of a calf (32:4). The Hebrew term *calf* means "young bull in his first strength." Bull images were common in Near Eastern religion, including both Egypt's and Canaan's. "The sacredness of the bull as the symbol of strength and reproductive power runs from Baal worship in Canaan to popular Hinduism in South India today, wherever religion is seen as a form of stockbreeder's 'fertility cult.'"[1]

Since it was later burned (see 32:20), the calf may have been a carved wooden statue covered with gold veneer. Or, it may have been crudely cast in solid gold, finished with a shaping tool, and later melted in the fire.[2]

Indulge in revelry (32:6). "Play" in NASB. The Hebrew verb has sexual connotations. Here it refers to the immoral sexual activity, such as orgies, that often accompanied fertility rites. This was one of the practices that had roused the Lord to such wrath against the Canaanites that He planned to destroy them.[3]

Stiff-necked (32:9). The Lord is comparing Israel to unresponsive oxen or horses who won't obey His pull on their yoke.

142

4. Realizing he had done wrong, how did Aaron try to redeem the situation (see 32:5)?

_____

_____

_____

_____

For Thought and Discussion: Why do you suppose God calls Israel "your people" (32:7) and "these people" (32:9) instead of "my people"?

5. To what extent did his attempt succeed (see 32:6), and why?

_____

_____

_____

_____

6. How did God evaluate the situation and those involved in it (see 32:7-10)?

_____

_____

_____

_____

7. God promised Abraham that He would destroy the wicked Canaanites and make Abraham into a great nation (see Genesis 12:2; 15:13-21). What do you think were His motives in making a similar offer to Moses (see 32:10)?

_____

_____

_____

_____

8. What reasons did Moses give for turning this offer down (see 32:11-13)?

Relent (32:12). The Scriptures are full of exhortations for men to turn from their sin to God, but here Moses pleads with the Lord to "repent" (KJV)! How can we correctly understand Moses' plea? First the "evil" (KJV) or "disaster" (NIV) to which Moses refers is not "sin" (God cannot sin, because sin is rebellion against God's character and will), but the terrible judgment that the Israelites deserve because of their idolatry. Second, the "repentance" Moses seeks from the Lord is simply the decision to accept his intercession on the people's behalf rather than executing divine justice. "The meaning is not that God changed His mind; still less that He regretted something that He intended to do. It means, in biblical language, that He now embarked on a different course of action from that already suggested as a possibility . . . God's promises and warnings are always conditional on man's response [see Jeremiah 18:7-10] . . . We are not to think of Moses as altering God's purpose toward Israel by this prayer, but as carrying it out: Moses was never more like God in these moments, for he shared God's mind and loving purpose."[4]

---

9. Once he descended from the mountain, how did Moses' reaction to Israel's sin compare with the Lord's (see 32:10,19)?

144

_____

_____

_____

_____

For Thought and Discussion: Why do you think Moses ground the gold up and made Israel drink it (see 32:20)?

10. Why was it appropriate that Moses broke the tablets of the Law?

_____

_____

_____

_____

_____

For Thought and Discussion: What extreme action was finally necessary to break the hold of the idolatrous worship on the people (see 32:25-29)? Why?

11. Moses didn't even try to offer a sacrifice to atone for such gross idolatry. How did he seek to make atonement (see 32:31-32)?

_____

_____

_____

_____

For Thought and Discussion: a. Why could Moses' prayer in 32:31-32 be considered his supreme act of intercession?

b. How does this prayer contrast with what had been God's original offer to him (see 32:10)?

12. "To intercede" means literally "to stand between." Psalm 106:23 describes Moses' actions in Exodus 32:11-14,31-32 as standing "in the breach." The imagery is of standing in a hole in a wall to prevent enemies from entering, or of standing astride a chasm between two cliffs, bridging the gap between God and man.
    What do you learn about intercession or standing in the breach from Exodus 32:11-14,31-32?

_____

_____

_____

_____

For Further Study:
On the Levite's zeal in Exodus 32:25-29, see Moses' command to all Israel in Deuteronomy 13:1-18.

Optional Application: Are you drastically committed to the Lord (see Luke 14:25-35)? How are you showing it? Does your situation call for the harshness of Exodus 32:25-29, or some other expression of putting the Lord ahead of even family ties and personal goals?

For Thought and Discussion: If Moses' intercession was successful, why was so much death and mourning also necessary (see 32:25-29,33-35)?

13. How does Moses' example show what it means that Jesus "always lives to intercede for [us]" (Hebrews 7:25)?

_____

_____

_____

_____

_____

14. Besides Moses' intercession, what else was necessary to heal the breach in the relationship between Israel and the Lord (see 32:25-29,35; 33:1-6)?

_____

_____

_____

_____

_____

Your response

15. What truth from 32:1–33:6 would you most like to take to heart?

_____

_____

_____

_____

_____

16. How would you like this to affect your thoughts and habits?

_____

_____

_____

_____

_____

_____

17. What action can you take to begin this process?

_____

_____

_____

_____

18. List any questions you have about 32:1–33:6.

_____

_____

_____

_____

_____

For the group

Warm-up. Ask group members to recall the last time they observed someone sinning against the Lord. Give them a minute, then ask them to answer this question aloud: "How did you react? What were your feelings and actions?" This may help members compare themselves to Moses in chapter 32.

Questions. This lesson is called "Idolatry and Intercession" because it focuses on these two issues. You can choose to discuss either or both of them. Decide whether your group seems most in need of ridding itself of idolatry, or most in need of learning to intercede for others with compassion born of identifying with the sinner. Which error most tempts your group: worldliness, self-righteousness, or both?

Prayer. Thank God that Jesus always lives to intercede for you. Ask Him to forgive your idolatry and to cleanse it from your lives. Pray for anyone, including each other, who is in the grip of sin.

1. R. A. Cole, *Exodus* (Downers Grove, IL: InterVarsity, 1973), 214.
2. Umberto Cassuto, *A Commentary of the Book of Exodus* (Jerusalem: The Magnes Press, 1967), 412; Kenneth Barker, ed., *The NIV Study Bible* (Grand Rapids, MI: Zondervan, 1985), 133.
3. J. J. Davis, *Moses and the Gods of Egypt* (Grand Rapids, MI: Baker, 1971), 285.
4. Cole, 217.

EXODUS 33:7–40:38
The Glory of the Lord

The Lord desired to dwell among His people. As you read 33:7–40:38, think about the lengths to which He went to enable men to know Him intimately and have Him among them.

Moses and the Lord (33:7–34:35)

1. Describe the relationship between Moses and the Lord (see 33:7-11).

_____

_____

_____

_____

_____

Tent of meeting (33:7). Not the tabernacle (it had not yet been erected), but a temporary structure. It was set up outside the camp as a place of revelation and communion between Moses and the Lord until the tabernacle was built.

Glory (33:18). The manifestation of God's essential nature. The pillar of cloud and fire was a visible appearance of God's glory; Moses wanted to see God even more deeply.

For Further Study:
Moses' unique privilege (see Exodus 33:11) is also emphasized in Deuteronomy 34:10. How do these passages enrich the significance of what Jesus says in John 16:12-17?

For Thought and Discussion:
  a. Did Moses use his relationship with God for his own advantage or for others' (see 32:11-13; 33:12-13; 34:8-9)? Explain.
  b. Do you use your relationship with God to make yourself feel secure and blessed, or for others' benefit? Pray about this.

149

For Thought and Discussion: What further do you learn about intercession from 33:12-16; 34:8-9?

For Thought and Discussion: God grants Moses' request partly because He "know[s Moses] by name" (33:17). What does this mean?

Optional Application: Does 34:5-7 move you to bow down and worship the Lord in awe (see 34:8)? Why or why not?

2. What desires does Moses express to God in 33:12-16?

_____

_____

_____

_____

3. Do you think these are wise or foolish desires? Why?

_____

_____

_____

_____

4. How has Moses gained the Lord's pleasure so much that his request to see God is granted (see 33:17)?

_____

_____

_____

_____

5. Read 34:6-8 aloud to yourself to let it have its full impact on you.

6. The glowing cloud was a visible expression of God's glory. Yet, what do you perceive about God's essential nature when He proclaims "his name" (character, identity) to Moses in 34:6-8?

_____

_____

_____

_____

150

Making a covenant (34:10). Renewing the covenant already made. Verses 10-26 repeat almost verbatim commands from chapters 20–24. These verses are often called the Ritual Decalogue because they can be easily divided into ten sections.

No one will covet your land (34:24). Attending the three annual festivals would require Israelite men to abandon their farms for days. They would have to trust the Lord to prevent animals and thieves from stealing their produce or even taking over their land. As it turned out, many Israelites decided it was folly to leave their possessions vulnerable while they went off to worship the Lord; economic prosperity could not be risked.

7. In renewing His covenant with Israel after the breach made by idolatry, God states ten instructions (see 34:11-26). With what dimension of life are they concerned?

_____

_____

_____

8. Since He had already revealed these regulations, why do you think He repeated them now?

_____

_____

_____

_____

_____

9. What did seeing God's glory do to Moses, and why (see 34:29-35)?

_____

_____

_____

Optional Application: God promised to protect and prosper His people if they were selfless in their worship and service of Him (see 34:24). Does this condition apply to you? Are you willing to let the Lord take care of your economic needs while you focus on serving Him? How can you improve your dedication to the Lord in worship and service?

For Thought and Discussion:
a. How does 34:29-35 indicate the complete restoration of fellowship between the Lord and Israel?
b. Without someone like Moses, do you think restoration would have occurred? Why or why not?

For Thought and Discussion: What similarities and differences do you see between Moses' dialogues with the Lord in chapters 32–34 and in chapters 3–4?

For Further Study:
Compare 34:29-35 to
2 Corinthians 3:4-18.
Is your ministry like
what Paul describes?
Why or why not?

**For Thought and
Discussion:** How
was the construction
of the tabernacle a
joint divine-human
project?

**Optional
Application:** How
does your enthusiasm
for giving your time
and possessions to
God's work compare
with Israel's? Do
you need to make
changes in this area?

**For Thought and
Discussion:** Why do
you suppose the Lord
repeats the Sabbath
law after His instruc-
tions for building
the tabernacle (see
31:12-17), again in
the Ritual Decalogue
(see 34:21), and again
before recounting the
building of the tab-
ernacle (see 35:1-3)?
Why was the Sabbath
so important, and
how was it relevant
to the tabernacle's
construction?

The tabernacle built and inhabited
(35:1–40:38)

10. After the debacle with the golden calf was dealt
with, Moses relayed all the Lord's instructions
about the tabernacle. With what spirit did the
Israelites respond to the call for precious materials and skilled workers (see 35:20–36:7)?

_____

_____

_____

_____

11. Why do you think 35:4–39:43 largely repeats
the specifications in 25:1–31:11, and even
includes details of measurements, quantities of
materials, and so on?

_____

_____

_____

_____

12. What blessings did Israel receive as a result of
obedience regarding the tabernacle (see 39:43;
40:34-38)?

_____

_____

_____

_____

_____

152

13. What contrast do you see between chapters 35–40 and chapter 32?

_____

_____

_____

_____

_____

14. Why do you think the book of Exodus ends — climaxes — with 40:34-38?

_____

_____

_____

_____

Your response

15. How is 33:7–40:38 relevant to your life?

_____

_____

_____

_____

16. How would you like to respond in prayer and action this week?

_____

_____

_____

_____

For Thought and Discussion: a. Why do you think the text so minutely lists the articles made (see 39:32-41)?
b. Why is the setting up of the tabernacle described in such detail (see 40:1-33)?

For Thought and Discussion: In what sense does the presence of God depend on the willingness and welcome extended to Him by men?

Optional Application: What do you need to do to make it possible for God to dwell intimately with you?

17. List any questions you have about 33:7–40:38.

_____

_____

_____

_____

_____

For the group

Warm-up. This lesson covers six chapters, but the common thread is the Lord manifesting His glory among His people—first with Moses, then in the tabernacle. Ask group members to tell how they have experienced God's presence during the past week. Of course, some members may answer "I haven't." That is okay, but plan to pray about it at the end of your meeting.

Read aloud. Instead of trying to read all of 33:7–40:38, just read 33:7–34:10 and 40:34-38.

Prayer. Use 34:6-8 as a springboard to praising the Lord for who He is. Ask Him to reveal His glory to each of you.

REVIEW

Now that you have worked through all of Exodus, take some time to pull together what you have studied. In the course of this review, you may want to look back at previous lessons and reread sections of the book. Ask the Lord to recall to your mind what He wants you to remember.

1. In lesson 1, we talked about four areas in which God transformed Israel through the events recorded in Exodus.

   a. How did He multiply Israel from a family into a nation (see 1:1-7; 12:38)?

   _____

   _____

   _____

   b. What steps did He take to change Israel from human slaves to divine servants?

   _____

   _____

   _____

   _____

   _____

   _____

For Thought and Discussion: What contrasts do you observe between the beginning and end of Exodus?

For Thought and Discussion: Which divine attributes and actions are emphasized in relation to . . .
   • Pharaoh and the Egyptians?
   • the Israelites?
   • Moses?

For Thought and Discussion: How does what Exodus teaches about the Lord compare with the way the Gospels portray Christ?

c. How much of the journey from Egypt to Canaan was accomplished by the end of Exodus?

_____

_____

d. Describe in general how God altered Israel's worship of and doctrine about Himself.

_____

_____

_____

_____

_____

_____

2. How does Exodus display each of the following attributes of God?

His power _____

_____

_____

_____

_____

_____

His faithfulness _____

_____

_____

_____

_____

_____

His uniqueness _____

_____

_____

_____

_____

_____

His exclusiveness or jealousy_____

_____

_____

_____

_____

His holiness _____

_____

_____

_____

_____

_____

His desire for intimacy with humans _____

_____

_____

_____

_____

_____

_____

For Thought and Discussion: What signs of spiritual progress, if any, does Israel show by the end of Exodus?

For Thought and Discussion:

a. How did Moses' forty years of keeping sheep help prepare him to follow the Lord and lead Israel through the wilderness? (Think of both practical and spiritual ways.)

b. How did Moses' experiences change him from a scared, defeated shepherd into a man who radiated God's glory and could speak to Him face-to-face? Which choices and experiences were most influential, and how?

His grace and mercy _____

_____

_____

_____

_____

_____

_____

_____

3. What do you learn about human nature from the Israelites, Egyptians, and Moses?

_____

_____

_____

_____

_____

_____

4. From the example of people in the book, what inner choices and outer circumstances seem to foster spiritual growth?

_____

_____

_____

_____

_____

_____

_____

5. From the behavior of Pharaoh, the Egyptians, Moses, and the Israelites, what would you say can frustrate or even reverse a person's (or group's) spiritual growth?

_____

_____

_____

_____

_____

_____

6. What are some ways in which Exodus helps you understand Christ's work?

_____

_____

_____

_____

_____

_____

7. Have you noticed any ways (thoughts, attitudes, opinions, behavior) in which you have changed as a result of studying Exodus? If so, describe how you have changed.

_____

_____

_____

_____

_____

_____

For Thought and Discussion:
   a. How are the Ten Commandments relevant to Christians today?
   b. What important insights can Christians learn from the instructions about the tabernacle and Israel's worship?

Optional Application: Identify a characteristic of Moses that you feel you need to develop. Try to understand how God developed it in Moses, and ask Him to help you cultivate it in your own life.

For Further Study:
Try outlining all of
Exodus. Then, com-
pare your outline to
one in a Bible ency-
clopedia, dictionary,
or commentary.

For Further Study:
Compare Acts 7:17-44
with Hebrews 11:23-29,
both of which draw
lessons from Exodus.
How do the empha-
ses of these two pas-
sages compliment
each other?

8. Look back through the study at questions in
   which you expressed a desire to make some
   personal application. Are you satisfied with your
   follow-through? Are there any areas you would
   like to continue to concentrate on? Pray about
   this, and jot any thoughts and plans here.

   _____

   _____

   _____

   _____

   _____

   _____

9. Reread any questions you wrote down at the
   end of each lesson. Do any important ones
   remain unanswered? If so, record them here,
   and plan ways to seek answers.

   _____

   _____

   _____

   _____

For the group

Reviewing a book can be vague and general because
people remember it only dimly or have difficulty
tying details together to see the big picture. Review
can also be a dull rehash of what people feel they
have already learned.

On the other hand, it can be an exciting chance
to see the story as God sees it, as a whole. The keys
to achieving this latter situation are the attitudes of
the leader and the group. The leader needs to moti-
vate the group to want to see the "God's-eye" view.
He or she needs to encourage members who find it
hard to connect ideas from many chapters. He or
she must also urge the group to think deeply when
quick answers seem to say everything easily. At the

same time, each group member needs to discipline himself to think and pray more deeply.

Warm-up. It might be motivating to ask, "What is the most exciting thing you have learned about God during the past four months from studying Exodus?" Or, try last lesson's warm-up again: "What aspects of God did each of you experience this week? How did God make His presence known to you this week?"

Questions. Try to split your time evenly between reviewing the content of the book (questions 1 through 6) and assessing how you have applied and want to apply it (questions 7 and 8). Also give everyone a chance to ask about anything they still don't understand (question 9). Encourage group members, rather than the leader, to suggest or find answers so that the group will grow less dependent on the leader.

Dividing your time like this may mean that you will not be able to discuss all the content questions in equal depth. You may need to choose a few questions to discuss thoroughly. Questions 7 and 8 deserve a large portion of your time because one of your most important functions as a group is to help each other apply God's Word to your lives. This should not be a time to try to impress each other, but a time to be honest. If you haven't changed much, say so. If you find application difficult, say so. On the other hand, if your lives have been shaken, say so. When you review applications, try not to let members compare their growth to each other's or to focus on guilt and failure. If anyone feels he has not obeyed God or grown much, you can discuss whether that is true and how the person can approach the situation from now on. Strive to encourage one another.

Evaluation. You might set aside a whole meeting to evaluate your study of Exodus and plan where to go next. Here are some questions you might consider:

How well did the study help you grasp the book of Exodus?
What did you like best about your meetings?
What did you like least? What would you change, and how?
How well did you meet the goals you set at your first meeting?

What did you learn about small-group study?
How could you practice together something you
     learned from your study?
What are the members' current needs? What will
     you do next?

Worship. Praise God for revealing Himself to you
through the book of Exodus. Thank Him for what
He is doing in each of your lives. Ask Him to guide
you as to where you should go from here.

STUDY AIDS

For further information on the material covered in this study, consider the following sources. They can be purchased at such websites as www.christianbook.com and www.amazon.com, or your local Christian bookstore should be able to order any of them if it does not carry them. Most seminary libraries have them, as well as many university and public libraries. If a source is out of print, you might be able to find it online.

Commentaries on Exodus

Cole, R. A. *Exodus* (InterVarsity, Tyndale Old Testament Commentary, 1973).
    This work is serious and succinct. In spite of the fact that it was first published a quarter of a century ago, it remains an excellent place to begin further study of Exodus.

Durham, John I. *Exodus* (Word, 1987).
    Durham bases his comments on his own translation of the Hebrew text. He discusses textual problems in the manuscripts and refers often to the original language. At the same time, this work does not require a seminary education to understand or profit from its many valuable insights. Durham is an evangelical, but does accept some of the so-called critical opinions concerning Exodus and the process by which the book supposedly reached its present state.

Gispen, W. H. *Exodus* (Zondervan, 1982).
    Gispen is a Dutch scholar in the conservative reformed tradition. His commentary is longer than Cole's, examining the text in more detail.

Histories, concordances, dictionaries, and handbooks

A *history* or *survey* traces Israel's history from beginning to end, so that you can see where each biblical event fits. *A Survey of Israel's History* by Leon

Wood (Zondervan, 1970) is a good basic introduction for laymen from a conservative viewpoint. Not critical or heavily learned, but not simplistic. Many other good surveys are also available. On the Persian period, serious students will enjoy *History of the Persian Empire* by A. T. Olmstead (University of Chicago, 1948). Also, Herodotus's *Histories* are available in English translation from several publishers.

A *concordance* lists words of the Bible alphabetically along with each verse in which the word appears. It lets you do your own word studies. An *exhaustive* concordance lists every word used in a given translation, while an *abridged* or *complete* concordance omits either some words, some occurrences of the word, or both.

Two of the three best exhaustive concordances are the venerable *Strong's Exhaustive Concordance* and Young's *Analytical Concordance to the Bible*. Both are available based on the *King James Version* and the *New American Standard Bible*. Strong's has an index in which you can find out which Greek or Hebrew word is used in a given English verse (although its information is occasionally outdated). *Young's* breaks up each English word it translates. Neither concordance requires knowledge of the original languages.

Perhaps the best exhaustive concordance currently on the market is *The NIV Exhaustive Concordance*. It features a Hebrew-to-English and a Greek-to-English lexicon (based on the eclectic text underlying the NIV), which are also keyed to *Strong's* numbering system.

Among other good, less expensive concordances, *Cruden's Complete Concordance* is keyed to the *King James* and *Revised Versions*, and the *NIV Complete Concordance* is keyed to the *New International Version*. These include all references to every word included, but they omit "minor" words. They also lack indexes to the original languages.

A *Bible dictionary* or *Bible encyclopedia* alphabetically lists articles about people, places, doctrines, important words, customs, and geography of the Bible.

The New Bible Dictionary, edited by J. D. Douglas, F. F. Bruce, J. I. Packer, N. Hillyer, D. Guthrie, A. R. Millard, and D. J. Wiseman (Tyndale, 1982) is more comprehensive than most dictionaries. Its 1,300 pages include quantities of information along with excellent maps, charts, diagrams, and an index for cross-referencing.

Unger's Bible Dictionary by Merrill F. Unger (Moody, 1979) is equally good and is available in an inexpensive paperback edition.

The Zondervan Pictorial Encyclopedia edited by Merrill C. Tenney (Zondervan, 1975, 1976) is excellent and exhaustive, and has been revised and updated. Its five 1,000-page volumes represent a significant financial investment, however, and all but very serious students may prefer to use it at a church, public college, or seminary library.

Unlike a Bible dictionary in the above sense, *Vine's Expository Dictionary of New Testament Words* by W. E. Vine (various publishers) alphabetically lists major words used in the *King James Version* and defines each New Testament Greek word that the KJV translates with its English word. Vine's also lists verse references where that Greek word appears, so you can do your own cross-references and word studies without knowing any Greek.

Vine's is a good, basic book for beginners, but it is much less complete than other Greek helps for English speakers. More serious students might prefer *The New International Dictionary of New Testament Theology*, edited by Colin Brown (Zondervan) or *The Theological Dictionary of the New Testament* by Gerhard Kittel and Gerhard Friedrich, abridged in one volume by Geoffrey W. Bromiley (Eerdmans).

A *Bible atlas* can be a great aid to understanding what is going on in a book of the Bible and how geography affected events. Here are a few good choices:

The Macmillan Atlas by Yohanan Aharoni and Michael Avi-Yonah (Macmillan, 1968, 1977) contains 264 maps, 89 photos, and 12 graphics. The many maps of individual events portray battles, movements of people, and changes of boundaries in detail.

The New Bible Atlas by J. J. Bimson and J. P. Kane (Tyndale, 1985) has 73 maps, 34 photos, and 34 graphics. Its evangelical perspective, concise and helpful text, and excellent research make it a very good choice, but its greatest strength lies in outstanding graphics, such as cross-sections of the Dead Sea.

The Bible Mapbook by Simon Jenkins (Lion, 1984) is much shorter and less expensive than most other atlases, so it offers a good first taste of the usefulness of maps. It contains 91 simple maps, very little text, and 20 graphics. Some of the graphics are computer-generated and intriguing.

The Moody Atlas of Bible Lands by Barry J. Beitzel (Moody, 1984) is scholarly, evangelical, and full of theological text, indexes, and references. This admirable reference work will be too deep and costly for some, but Beitzel shows vividly how God prepared the land of Israel perfectly for the acts of salvation He planned to accomplish in it.

A *handbook* of biblical customs can also be useful. Some good ones are *Today's Handbook of Bible Times and Customs* by William L. Coleman (Bethany, 1984) and the less detailed *Daily Life in Bible Times* (Nelson, 1982).

For small-group leaders

The Small Group Leader's Handbook by Steve Barker et al. (InterVarsity, 1982).

Written by an InterVarsity small group with college students primarily in mind. It includes information on small-group dynamics and how to lead in light of them, and many ideas for worship, building community, and outreach. It has a good chapter on doing inductive Bible study.

Em Griffin. *Getting Together: A Guide for Good Groups* (InterVarsity, 1982).

Applies to all kinds of groups, not just Bible studies. From his own experience, Griffin draws deep insights into why people join groups; how people relate to each other; and principles of leadership, decision making, and discussions. It is fun to read, but its 229 pages will take more time than the above book.

You Can Start a Bible Study Group by Gladys Hunt (Harold Shaw, 1984).
Builds on Hunt's thirty years of experience leading groups. This book is wonderfully focused on God's enabling. It is both clear and applicable for Bible study groups of all kinds.

How to Build a Small-Groups Ministry by Neal F. McBride (NavPress, 1994).
This hands-on workbook for pastors and lay leaders includes everything you need to know to develop a plan that fits your unique church. Through basic principles, case studies, and worksheets, McBride leads you through twelve logical steps for organizing and administering a small-groups ministry.

How to Lead Small Groups by Neal F. McBride (NavPress, 1990).
Covers leadership skills for all kinds of small groups—Bible study, fellowship, task, and support groups. Filled with step-by-step guidance and practical exercises to help you grasp the critical aspects of small-group leadership and dynamics.

Bible study methods

Braga, James. *How to Study the Bible* (Multnomah, 1982).
Clear chapters on a variety of approaches to Bible study: synthetic, geographical, cultural, historical, doctrinal, practical, and so on. Designed to help the ordinary person without seminary training to use these approaches.

Fee, Gordon, and Douglas Stuart. *How to Read the Bible for All Its Worth* (Zondervan, 1982).
After explaining in general what interpretation and application are, Fee and Stuart offer chapters on interpreting and applying the different kinds of writing in the Bible: Epistles, Gospels, Old Testament Law, Old Testament narrative, the Prophets, Psalms, Wisdom, and Revelation. Fee and Stuart also suggest good commentaries on each biblical book. They write as evangelical scholars who personally recognize Scripture as God's Word for their daily lives.

Jensen, Irving L. *Independent Bible Study* (Moody, 1963), and *Enjoy Your Bible* (Moody, 1962).
The former is a comprehensive introduction to the inductive Bible study method, especially the use of synthetic charts. The latter is a simpler introduction to the subject.

Wald, Oletta. *The Joy of Discovery in Bible Study* (Augsburg, 1975).
Wald focuses on issues such as how to observe all that is in a text, how to ask questions of a text, how to use grammar and passage structure to see the writer's point, and so on. Very helpful on these subjects.